AF406507

Go On! Be Your Own Boss

A complete step-by-step guide to starting a business

Go On! Be Your Own Boss

A complete step-by-step guide to starting a business

Anthony Wilkinson

First edition—2024

Pen-2-Paper

www.pen-2-paper.co.uk

While every precaution has been taken in the preparation of this book, the publisher assumes no responsibility for errors or omissions, or for damages resulting from the use of the information contained herein.

Go On! Be Your Own Boss

First Edition: May 1, 2024

Copyright © 2024 Pen-2-Paper, 86-90 Paul Street, London, EC2A 4NE

www.pen-2-paper.co.uk

Written by Anthony Wilkinson

Contents

About the Author

Throughout his working life, Anthony Wilkinson has been involved in organisational development across many industries. He has a natural flair for improvement and an instinct to identify where effective changes would be beneficial; Anthony has successfully transformed many leading organisations.

As a teenager, Anthony wanted to be a design engineer. Through his determination and support from his teachers, the dream became a reality. As a newly-qualified design draughtsman, Anthony soon realised he wanted more from life. After a further spell in full-time education, he embarked upon a successful career in corporate development.

In this book, Go On! Be Your Own Boss, Anthony shares his knowledge, expertise, and experience of planning, starting, and running a business to make the journey from employment to self-employment quick and painless.

By following the examples in this book and creating detailed business and marketing plans, Anthony guides the reader step-by-step through a complex network of tasks and into a successful new venture.

*The business planning process begins with
the statement of the objective and ends with
the achievement of the objective.*

Preface

Around 15% of the UK labour force is self-employed.

Self-employment often provides flexible working and higher personal rewards.

By following the simple step-by-step guidelines in this book, you can make the leap from the routine of employment to the freedom of self-employment.

The book is mainly aimed at people in the UK who are keen to become self-employed.

Use the book as a guide working from front to back or as a reference book, dipping into the relevant section using the contents list.

Credits

Cover	Y Akin, Unsplash
Planning your business	WordItOut
Limited Company/Partnership	R Gomez, Unsplash
Alternative sources of income	P Veater, Unsplash
Where will the business . . .?	M Blan, Unsplash
Networking	A Grubnyak, Unsplash
Payment policy	Nupixen, Unsplash
Elevator Pitch	LuismiCSS, Pixabay
Design a logo	Y Duanmu, Unsplash
Code of Conduct	M Mardani, Unsplash

Dedications

Special thanks to my mother, brother, and sister.

In a unique way, each provides inspiration and support.

Acknowledgments

I believe I learned something good or bad from everyone I ever worked with.

So, even though I can't remember all the names, I thank you.

How to use this book

Go On! Be Your Own Boss guides the reader through the often-confusing choices they need to make as they consider self-employment . . . and the transition from employment.

The book provides a logical step-by-step approach to planning, setting up, and running the business.

Initially, the book focuses on the business plan. It shows how the plan develops into a thriving, fully-fledged operation, providing easy-to-follow guidance at every step, from deciding on the type of business to building a website.

In Chapter Three, we spend time looking at the details of the business plan, helping make those crucial decisions.

In Chapter Four, we turn those plans into action. So, instead of assessing the various types of business bank accounts, we open one. The chapter also kickstarts the marketing activity, website design, social media, networking, etc.

Chapter Five then explains how to run the business successfully, tackling such topics as invoicing, marketing, banking, etc.

With clear descriptions and guidance on every aspect of planning, establishing, and running a new business, the book is intended as a guide and a reference to help the reader become self-employed.

Introduction

In the UK, anyone can become self-employed as long as they register for self-assessment with the tax authorities. There are an estimated 4.25 million independent workers in the UK.

Self-employment often provides opportunities and benefits not ordinarily available through an employer. Those benefits can include higher rates of pay, non-standard working hours, and flexible holidays; often, it's the flexibility that encourages employees to go self-employed.

However, regular employment usually carries other benefits that can be overlooked by someone looking at self-employment for the first time. An employer's benefits package might include childcare allowance, sick pay, medical insurance, paid holidays, a company car, a pension, etc. The value and convenience of those benefits are enormous and shouldn't be ignored.

Other aspects of self-employment must also be considered, such as social isolation, the risk of poor work/life balance, the lack of access to knowledge and news, and the peaks and troughs of the workload (and the income). It's great when the money is coming in, except that you're too busy to do anything but work. Suddenly, the work stops because you didn't do enough marketing; now, there's no money coming in. Those lean times must be managed to guarantee a steady income.

This book assesses the benefits and agonies of self-employment. It looks at strategies to address the elements that make self-employment secure, beneficial, and enjoyable.

retailing
accounting
marketing
educating
assessing
treating
repairing
heating
helping
delivering
writing
fabricating
guarding
cooking
metalworking
lifting
fitting
loaning
insuring
servicing
acting
testing
editing
gardening
advising
washing
building
hairdressing
teaching
bookkeeping
freezing
singing
training
hiring
growing
driving
spraying
reporting
tutoring
demolishing
auditing
baking
buying
caring
shopping
engineering

ONE:
WHAT DO SELF-EMPLOYED PEOPLE DO?

Generally, a self-employed person provides something—skill, product, knowledge, service, expertise—that doesn't already exist, such as:

- An extra pair of hands to do a task
- Products or equipment that are needed: software, food, etc.
- Skills to tackle a tricky problem
- Expertise in finding a solution
- Teaching, training, or mentoring
- New activities, products, or processes

Typically, a self-employed person will do something they're good at, or love doing—ideally both!

Equally, whatever they do must be saleable . . . and ultimately profitable. In other words, the goods or services must be needed by people or organisations that are willing to pay—the customers.

As the term implies, self-employed people work for themselves in supplying others. However, as we'll see in Chapter 2, doing the business is not the same as running the business—being good at baking, for example, isn't the same as being good at bookkeeping or marketing.

Self-employed people are typically contractors, consultants, freelancers, or sole proprietors delivering a vast range of products or services. For example, they MUST understand what the customer needs most and provide the best solutions.

They MUST be better than the rest, not just in knowledge and expertise, but also in performance, service levels, reporting, listening, and being a vital effective part of the customer's team/family/community/workforce.

Here's a short list of some of the activities self-employed people do:

Advising, accounting, acting, advertising, auditing

Baking, bookkeeping, brokering, building, buying

Caring, cleaning, converting, cooking, counselling

Dancing, delivering, demolishing, designing, diving

Editing, educating, engineering, entertaining

Fabricating, farming, fishing, fitting, fixing, freezing

Gardening, grooming, growing, guarding, guiding

Hairdressing, heating, helping, hiring, hosting

Inspecting, installing, insuring, investigating, ironing

Lending, letting, lifting, lighting, loading, loaning

Making, mapping, marketing, mediating, metalworking

Painting, photographing, playing, printing, publishing

Recruiting, removing, repairing, reporting, researching

Servicing, shopping, singing, spraying, surveying

Teaching, tending, testing, trading, training, treating

Washing, woodworking, writing

and so on.

Self-employed people shouldn't try to do everything—they MUST concentrate on providing the solutions the customer needs.

They MUST stick to the agreement and, in particular, avoid the temptation to stray into areas where they don't have the levels of knowledge, skills, and experience required to do the task correctly.

Follow the Code of Conduct—Annex A.

Above all, a self-employed person offers professionalism, which can be defined by these values:

- Behaviour—objective, diligent, and caring
- Product/Service—lawful and honest
- Transparent—open and accountable
- Efficient—optimising time and resources
- Quality—providing excellence
- Confidential—protecting sensitive information
- Responsible—owning the decisions, actions, and consequences
- Flexible—agile and able to change
- Assurance—a safe pair of hands
- Reliable—a consistent approach.

Self-employed people are often more flexible and adaptive than staff employed larger businesses; they are unhindered by corporate culture.

As a direct result of being self-employed, people can offer unique solutions, an independent approach, speedy responses, and expertise not available elsewhere.

DOING

RUNNING

TWO:
DOING AND RUNNING

Two distinct elements of a business must be considered by anyone going self-employed; 'doing the business AND running the business'

Doing the business is the part you're probably very good at; we'll call it your technical ability; those are the products, services, skills, knowledge, or expertise your customers will pay for.

Running the business is the part you might not be so good at and won't get paid for; we'll call it your management ability.

Management includes marketing, sales, monitoring, reporting, invoicing, banking, purchasing, record keeping, etc.

Being self-employed, you must do the business and run the business—you own the company, so don't neglect it.

At the outset, when the business becomes operational, most of your available time will be spent running the business—getting it off the ground.

As the work starts to come in and you begin to earn some money, the emphasis shifts towards doing the business. But you must still run the business, using as much as 20 or 30% of your time, which could be one day each week.

There's no point in working hard if you're not going to keep your customer records up to date or collect your income when agreed. So, in your dreams of going self-employed, consider DOING the business and RUNNING the business.

We'll delve into both of these elements as you work through setting up and launching your new venture.

Starting a new business can be an exciting, challenging, and daunting time. But, if you follow this guide, you will quickly understand how to start and run a successful business, which will provide the knowledge and confidence you require to become self-employed.

When thinking about setting up a business, most people start by drafting a business plan. A good business plan is essential; it helps you understand how the business will work. But it's not the first thing you should consider.

The first thing you should consider is how self-employment might impact your family, friends, lifestyle, hobbies . . . and your entire life.

You will not make lots of money from day one; you must build the business, which will take time. There are many considerations, such as your workplace, working hours, equipment, earnings, customers, etc.

So, before we look at the mechanics of setting up a business and preparing a good business plan, you must think about how your life will change when you are self-employed.

It's okay to think about the opportunity, but also think about the risk. For example, do you have a secure network of potential customers, or will you need to look for them? Do you have clearly defined products, services, skills, knowledge, or expertise that customers will buy?

Take your time to ponder; it's a big decision.

THREE:
PLANNING YOUR BUSINESS

Congratulations. By turning the page, I assume you have decided to look closer at becoming self-employed. This is where the hard work starts, so let's go through the following stages together—step-by-step.

Before the company can start operating, you must plan the business and begin to set it up—that's around 30 tasks to complete, which could take as much as 240 hours (the equivalent of working full-time for six weeks).

Don't rush to get the tasks finished; use the planning activity as an opportunity to learn and understand how your business will be structured and how it will operate. Some of those tasks will require tough decisions—don't guess, take advice, do some research, and get it right.

You can stop and rethink your decision to go self-employed at any point. Don't burn bridges or make financial commitments until you are sure it's what you want to do.

Create a Business Plan

We're going to start by creating a business plan . . . I know, it sounds boring!

However, this plan is structured so that we learn as we go along. It allows us to understand the business fully and informs us of our choices before making any decisions.

The more effort you put into the business plan, the more realistic the outcome will be. You will better understand your new business from a detailed, accurate plan before you start operating.

The business plan aims to capture the necessary information to make educated decisions. The business plan is for you; it must be realistic.

Whatever you tell your accountant or bank manager, you mustn't create a pretty business plan that gives YOU (or them) a false impression.

I've seen many business plans packed full of nonsense— their prime purpose is to create a positive impression for the reader; please don't do that to yourself—be pragmatic. No one else needs to see your business plan, so be honest and keep it real.

Within this chapter, we will develop a detailed business plan that will take around 40 hours, including the necessary research. Don't rush; there is no advantage in creating a flawed business plan quickly.

Then, in the next chapter, we will work through your business plan and turn it into a viable new business.

Decide on the company name

It sounds easy, right?

In reality, choosing a suitable name can be extremely difficult, and there are a few potential pitfalls you must avoid.

Obviously, if you want your company name to be memorable, it must be inventive. Shorter names of two syllables are easier to remember.

You might want to avoid using your name—Anthony Wilkinson Associates—since your potential customers won't find you easily unless they already know your name.

Why not combine two words or concepts, such as Facebook, YouTube or LinkedIn—all simple mashups? Also, a name starting with the letter A or a number will always appear at the beginning of any directory, so avoid names beginning with a letter from the end of the alphabet—unless it's memorable.

Avoid long names that are not in everyday use. I once came across a company called THAUMATURGY. Firstly, could you pronounce it? Secondly, would you remember it? Thirdly, could you spell it? Thaumaturgy means the art of doing the impossible—like magic.

Some people choose a name to describe what they do, AW Consultants, but is it really descriptive or memorable?

Let's have a look at different methods of creating company names.

Real names, such as Apple, Amazon, and Pandora, can't be descriptive; otherwise, they couldn't be used as a trademark. But real names are available off-the-shelf; choose one and own it. Misspellings like Fiverr, Flickr, and Google can also work, but be careful since misspellings could breach a trademark.

Compound names, such as FaceBook, FireFox, and YouTube, use two words to provide a more potential combination than using one name. Just find two short words and combine them. Compound names are trendy.

Phrases such as Last.fm, LinkedIn, and MySpace.

Phrases are similar to compound names, except the words make sense because they follow regular linguistic rules.

Blends, such as Deliveroo, Microsoft, and Wikipedia, are two-part names where both parts are recognisable terms; for example, MICROcomputer SOFTware becomes MICROSOFT.

Choosing a great name can be fun, but the name must pass two tests initially.

The first test is domain name availability; check your company name using a domain name website—try different TLDs (Top-Level Domains) such as .com, .net, .org, .co.uk, etc. If the name is already in use, try using a Thesaurus to find something similar, or split the domain name with a hyphen.

The second test is Company Name availability—especially where you want to set up a limited company or partnership. Obviously, the name must be unique, so it's worth checking if the company exists (even if you're setting up as a sole trader) to avoid duplication and potential confusion.

Company Names are registered with Companies House; go to the website and search for a Company Name.

Also, company names must avoid sensitive words, such as terms that imply a connection with Governments or use other regulated words. Examples include Accredited, Architect, Assembly, Association, Bank, Cabinet, Chamber, Charity, Chartered, Chemist, Commission, Education, Institute, International, Notary, Olympic, Paramedic, Therapist, etc. If in doubt over the eligibility of a company name, seek professional advice.

When you've thought of a great name, keep a note of it, don't rush out and start marketing it; there are many more crucial decisions to be made before then.

Determine the type of business

The kind of business you choose plays a massive part in how you will set it up. In essence, you have a choice of three types of business set up:

- Sole trader—you are self-employed
- Business partnership—you are self-employed with others
- Limited company/limited partnership—your company employs you

Let's have a look at each in turn and understand the details of each business type:

- **Sole Trader** – A sole trader is a self-employed individual. All profits are retained by the sole trader (after taxes have been paid). A sole trader is entirely responsible for the business, including any debts.

  Anyone who earns over £1,000 from self-employment must register for tax and file a tax return. You might also want to make voluntary Class 2 National Insurance payments, which help you qualify for benefits such as a state pension.

As a sole trader, you must maintain records of sales and expenses, and pay Income Tax on all profits. Sole traders must also include their name and business name on all correspondence, especially contracts, letters and invoices.

The business name of a sole trader cannot include the words limited, Ltd, LLP, or plc since this would be misleading. The name should not contain a sensitive word or expression—see more information on sensitive words in the previous section entitled 'Decide on the company name'.

Sole traders don't need to register their business but must register for tax. The critical element of being a sole trader is that net income is subject to income tax, so accounting for income and expenses is essential. Record ALL expenditure, as this will offset part of your tax bill.

- **Business partnership/limited partnership** – A business partnership is a partnership between individuals, limited companies, or both. The partners share all responsibilities and profits. A nominated partner manages the business records in a partnership, including the sales and expenses records.

  Each partner deals with their personal tax affairs. Business partnerships must also include the names of each partner and the business name on all correspondence, especially contracts, letters and invoices.

  Since this would be misleading, the partnership name cannot include the words limited, Ltd, LLP or plc. The name should not contain a sensitive word or expression—see more information on sensitive words in the previous section entitled 'Decide on the company name'.

All partnerships must register their business partnership, and each partner needs to register for tax. The critical element of being a partnership is that all net income is considered profit and subject to income tax—like a Sole Trader.

So, accounting for income and expenses is essential. Sometimes, the partnership may be incorporated by forming a limited partnership. In many respects, a business partnership is similar to being a sole trader. Likewise, limited partnerships are similar to a Limited Company.

- **Limited Company/Limited Partnership**

Technically, establishing a limited company is not self-employment. You will be working for the company and being paid a salary. However, with the meteoric rise of single-director companies, the option to form a limited company is included here for completeness.

A limited company is legally separate from the people who run it, which keeps the company finances apart from personal funds. The company is regulated under company law to ensure it operates within the legal framework. Statutory disclosures to Companies House confirm compliance. Such disclosures include:

- Statutory Accounts
- Confirmation Statement
- Any changes of Directors, Registered Office, and the Articles of Association

Limited Companies pay corporation tax on the taxable profits at a rate of 17% (at the time of writing). For businesses with high incomes, being a Limited Company has tax advantages. Likewise, those companies with high R&D expenditure can often take advantage of Government grants and tax credits.

Company tax rules are more complex than sole trader tax rules. A sole trader company is easy to start and maintain; limited companies have higher costs and more corporate filings to Companies House.

To establish a limited company, it must be registered with Companies House. Don't do this until you've made the big decision and you're absolutely committed to becoming self-employed.

Which to choose?

When considering self-employment, you must decide whether to set up as a sole trader, partnership, or limited company, alone or with a partner.

The main difference between being a sole trader and being a limited company is the taxation of profits, which depends on the income level.

Avoid a situation where you work freelance exclusively for one customer. While this arrangement has some tax benefits, the tax authorities may deem you employed. The rules around 'deemed employed' are complex and often force the customer to divulge to the tax authorities the nature of your relationship with them.

One test the tax authorities often undertake to determine 'deemed employed' is whether you are obliged to work within their regime or are free to refuse the work.

A similar test determines whether you have control over your work or it's under the customer's control. If the test proves you're under the customer's control, you might be 'deemed employed'. If you're unsure, get professional advice.

Consider your business type and if you've got any questions, make a note and discuss them with your accountant or bank when we get to that point.

Assess business bank account options

Selecting the right business bank account can be daunting, so it's best to start looking at the earliest opportunity. Sign-up for updates from the various providers and follow the comparison websites to see the latest deals.

A sole trader is not required to use a business bank account. But, using an account that is not your personal account is helpful to manage your business finances.

A limited company certainly needs a dedicated business bank account since the money belongs to the company, not the directors.

The range of business bank accounts is vast, each highlighting the particular features and benefits of the account. Some, for example, have free transactions, although these are usually time-limited offers.

Read the small print because some transactions may incur a charge—and the cost can be as high as £25 per transaction. Also, look for fixed bank fees, which are typically paid monthly. Those fixed fees can be as much as £40, even for a simple no-frills account.

Often, the banking deals sound unbelievable, but the small print reveals the full extent of the charges and fees, including fees for withdrawals and transfers.

Consider how you might use the bank and how often. As a consultant, for example, there won't be a lot of cash and coins. Most of the payments received will be by transfer, as might the costs going out. Consider whether you need a cheque book, for example, or an overdraft facility (check the rate first).

As a market trader, there could be a lot of cash—which has to be counted and bagged for the bank run. The bank could incur additional charges for dealing with cash.

I use Tide for my business account; it's inexpensive, straightforward, fast, and secure. Everything is online, so there are no extra charges for statements, etc. More on opening a business bank account later.

Start-up costs

Obviously, there is a load of costs that must be covered before you start to earn income.

One way to finance the cost is to dig into your savings, borrow money, or put the expenses on a credit card.

However you fund the costs, maintain a record, and keep receipts. It is essential to estimate the start-up costs to avoid surprises and obtain a complete picture of what upfront finances you might need.

The start-up costs might include:

- Premises rental
- Travel to meet potential customers or suppliers
- Website development
- Domain name registration
- Advertising, including press releases
- Company registration (incorporation)
- Insurance
- Office, accounting, and emailing software
- Business cards and brochures
- Communications—phone, internet, etc.
- Processing equipment—ovens (for a bakery), lawn mowers (for a gardener), welder (for a metalworker), van (for deliveries), etc
- Phone
- Materials and stock
- PC/Laptop and printer
- Desk, chair, etc.
- Complete the business plan, including the start-up timetable

We're almost at the point where you can start to decide whether you want to go self-employed; the choice should mainly be based on the content of the business plan. So, let's have a look at it.

A formatted copy of the business plan can be downloaded from the publisher's website:

https://www.pen-2-paper.co.uk/downloads.html.

The plan features guidance on each element of the business. Be realistic, truthful, and thorough as possible; fully understand the various choices and decisions.

Consider your answers against each of the elements. Make notes as you go along, which will help guide you toward self-employment. Be as specific as you can.

OK, ready? Here we go!

BUSINESS PLAN

1. What is the name of the Business?

We already considered the business name earlier in this Chapter. Make the name unique and memorable.

2. Business address.

All businesses need an address. The address must be quoted on all correspondence, especially contracts, letters, and invoices.

The business address could be a home address for a sole trader or partnership. However, some people prefer to keep the business address separate from their home address. A PO Box or mailbox might be a viable solution—check with Companies House or get professional advice.

Virtual mailboxes are an inexpensive option where the post is sent to a prominent city address, redirected to your home address, or stored for collection. Check the small print in the contract, especially the additional charges for handling mail.

Limited companies need a business address known as a Registered Office. Details of the Registered Office are available for anyone to view. Again, this can be a physical business address or a virtual office. Note that some virtual offices do not have Registered Office facilities. So, when incorporating your limited company, check that the virtual office provider has a Registered Office facility.

Research the options for your business address, but don't commit yet.

3. In which market/industry will the business operate?

Retail, Farming, Agriculture, Beverages, Construction, Business support, Professional services, Manufacturing, Food, Accommodation, Sport, Finance, Insurance, Real estate, Wholesale trade, Travel, Information technology, Art, Entertainment, Recreation, or Other, and so on.

Be clear about the market or industry in which you will operate. You are providing products or services, but is that your industry? What industry are your customers in?

This is an important point; it helps to focus your efforts on the needs of a particular market or industry.

If you're providing printed matter, for example, to the travel industry only, you're in the travel industry—you can target the travel industry confidently. But if you're providing printed matter to many industry sectors, you're in the printing industry and might not have the knowledge and expertise to tackle specific markets.

4. Consider your technical skills.

Are you qualified or experienced?

Do you have any specialist skills you could use? Are your skills unique?

Do you know things that other people don't?

5. What specifically will the business provide?

Potential customers must know what products or services you will provide; you must describe and convey what you can do for your customers.

Be very specific here, and be honest—do your customers need what you're offering, and will they pay for it?

6. Describe the goals and objectives of the business.

This is more of a personal question that forces you to think about the business objectives—to be the market leader, be sustainable, provide an income, have a large office, earn millions, make enough money to retire early, etc.

Be realistic; you're not going to conquer the world. So, what is the purpose of the business?

Also, think about your motivation—what are you getting out of this?

7. Describe the planned timeline for reaching the objectives.

Consider how long it's going to take to achieve your goals. Is it a short-term venture or a long-term investment? Again, be realistic.

I know it's difficult at such an early stage in the planning, but try to think ahead by three or more years.

8. Describe any plans to develop additional products and services.

Will you be able to sell the same products and services to the same customers forever?

Consider the future requirements of your customers and the market or industry. Maybe you could sell similar products and services to another industry or market. Think ahead by three or more years.

9. Describe the target market/industry of the business.

This question begins to define potential customers and helps you approach them. Where are they? Who are they? What are they doing?

It's time to do some research to find and describe your target market. Scour the internet, searching for potential customers.

Use keywords based on your knowledge and experience— only you know what those keywords are.

You may find that most of the research uncovers potential customers you already know—no surprises there.

Think about the products and services you will offer; why do these customers need your products or services?

10. What is the company vision?

The vision statement should be short, purposeful, encouraging and descriptive. It should declare what you want the business to achieve or become.

Without a vision, there can be no plan for the future. Aim for nine words maximum. TED, for example, has a simple vision, '*Spread ideas*'. TED uses the vision in its advertising.

Go back to check your goals and objectives—are they aligned with your vision?

When creating a vision, a good starting point is to consider how your business will change the world, society, or community.

11. How will you measure success?

It would help if you had targets so you can measure the success of what you're doing.

One measure of success might be income; you need shelter and food, so income is essential.

But what about work/life balance?

We'll do the maths later; for now, consider what success might look like.

12. Why do you want to be self-employed?

A soul-searching question.

You must understand your motivation.

Some like the idea of being the boss; others might want to prove a point; for some, it's about the money and the flexible hours.

Be honest; otherwise, you might not achieve your true ambition.

13. How much money do you NEED to earn?

This is a critical question—if you can't earn enough, the business won't survive.

Calculate the amount of money you need to cover your monthly personal expenses—mortgage, bills, car, loans, pension, insurance, food, clothing, utility bills, school fees, etc.

Check through your bank statements to calculate your outgoings.

Clearly state, 'I must earn xxxx every month'.

14. How much money do you WANT to earn?

A slightly different question—being realistic, specify the amount of money you want to make.

The answer to this question will determine how much work you need to do.

If, for example, you WANT to earn £8,000 a month and your daily rate is £400 (net), you must work 20 days doing the business.

Remember, you must do the business AND run the business—you must find time to do both. So, twenty days doing the business, plus four days running the business—that's 24 working days in a month.

15. Do you have any alternative sources of income?

Passive income may come from investments, property, book sales, etc.

Some people choose to become self-employed while continuing their current employment part-time. It reduces the risk and the financial burden—they're guaranteed an income. However, they don't devote all their efforts to their business adversely, so they may miss opportunities.

16. Are there any sources of funding to support you?

In the UK, there are many sources of funding for new business start-ups.

Check with the gov.uk website to discover what funding, support, and benefits are available, such as the New Enterprise Allowance scheme. A little research might be beneficial.

When I established Westwood Associates in 1997, I became aware of an Enterprise Allowance scheme operating in my region. The programme provided mandatory learning, which was highly beneficial.

Over six weeks, I attended courses on marketing, contracting, tendering, and many helpful topics. Additionally, I met some great people who were in exactly the same position as me. As a bonus, I was paid a weekly allowance to help me get established.

17. Type of business; Sole trader, Partnership, Limited Company.

We have already considered this, but we're getting closer to the decision time. You might decide to take professional advice.

When asked, I usually suggest going sole trader if the income is forecast to be under the VAT threshold. This approach has no logic; it just means any earnings forecast to be above the threshold will trigger VAT registration and possibly incorporation.

Sometimes, new startups might decide that a limited company has more prestige or credibility, making it easier to attract customers.

However, running a limited company means that additional legal requirements need to be met, such as the Annual General Meeting, Confirmation Statement, and Statutory Accounts—all properly administered and reported to Companies House.

Note. It's easy to go from sole trader to limited company, but not so easy to go the other way.

18. Who owns the business?

Be very clear about this. Is it just you, or you and your significant other, or you and a business partner?

This is crucial if you decide to incorporate (form a limited company) due to the responsibilities and liabilities of the Directors.

19. Describe the skills, experience, and qualifications of the owners.

Some think this is an odd question and struggle to understand its relevance.

Maybe the question should be, 'Do you have the skills, experience, and qualifications to do the business and run the business?

If not, what action will you take?'

We already assumed you have the technical skills to do the business. But, many people lack the additional skills needed to run the business. In fact, some fail to understand what is required to run the business.

You could employ the required skills in the form of a bookkeeper, a marketing agency, a salesperson, a website developer, etc. If that's your solution, ensure those costs are in your financial projections.

Alternatively, you could tap into the vast range of learning opportunities from leading universities and institutions.

You must have access to the knowledge, skills, experience, and qualifications to run the business.

20. Describe the structure of the business.

As a sole trader, this may be a simple question—you are the business. However, in the context of the previous question, how will you fulfil all the duties of running a business?

Consider employing professional support—accountant, solicitor, marketer, etc. Also, think about self-employed people in your network who might add value to your business by adding complementary services or may help you reduce the high workload demands.

For a limited company, the business structure can be similar to that of a sole trader. However, I would strongly recommend appointing an accountant, especially one who can steer you through the incorporation, which, although not complicated, has no margin for error. There could be more than one director in a limited company.

The structure and responsibilities must be defined.

21. How many staff does the business require?

This is an extension of the previous point. It's time to consider who does what and whether any staff will be needed—now or in the future.

Employing staff is a big step, as it can invoke employment law, health & safety law, pensions, income tax, national insurance, etc.

22. Where will the business operate?

The region where the business will operate is often not considered when creating the business plan. In fact, during the first few weeks or months, all income is welcomed.

But think about the whereabouts of your customers—how far are you able or willing to travel? Depending on your customers' services, it may be possible to service them remotely via the Internet.

You might decide some services are best-delivered face-to-face while others are best served online.

Providing products online might not be so easy, depending on the product type and its packaging.

23. Where will the business be located?

The physical location of your business could be significant. If you decide to work from home, the question is irrelevant unless you're willing to move home and be closer to potential customers.

Working from an office provides freedom from domestic distractions but often involves a commute.

Prestigious addresses are usually in big cities, which often means a rush hour commute.

Consider this: does the location of your business matter to your customers?

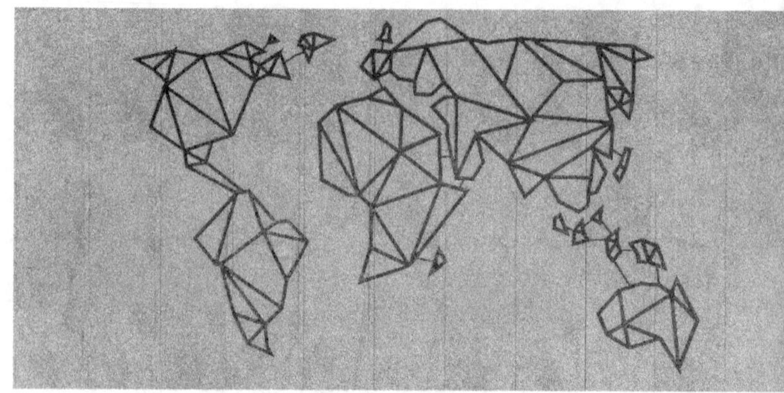

Weigh up the business location options very carefully.

From experience, I know the business location is often critical to business success, not from the desirable location but from the commute and easy customer access.

In 2000, I was appointed Corporate Development consultant to a start-up company in Bolton. I lived in Wakefield at the time.

The contract was for two days each week for five years. The commute wasn't a problem—a 120-mile roundtrip twice a week. Then, I got involved in quality management at the same company, which added another day each week.

Soon after, the company asked me to lead a Knowledge Transfer Partnership with Queens University Belfast, which added another day each week.

And so it continued until I was fully engaged as a consultant—40 hours each week with a 120 roundtrip commute every day (600 miles weekly). The 40-hour working week became 60+ hours including the commute.

The nature of my work meant that I had to be hands-on. The commute became a problem, so be aware of the location of your office in relation to your customers.

24. Does the location of the business provide an advantage?

To complete your decision-making on your business location, determine if moving closer to potential customers would make sense. By moving closer, would it be easier for you to serve their needs?

25. Describe the typical customers.

What will your customers want from you?

Gain a clear understanding of the potential customers in your chosen region.

Are they big companies or small companies? Do you have any experience of working with them? Do you know anyone who works for your potential customers?

Dig deep into the details of potential customers. Do some research; it will pay dividends.

26. Why will customers choose your business?

Marketers will often talk about the USP (Unique Sales Proposition) and why customers choose YOUR products and services over your competitors. I'm not going to disagree with the marketers.

However, I might have a slightly different view.

Your USP is … YOU!

29

When you're pitching to a customer—they see you. You are the one thing your competitors don't have.

Additionally, customers must know what you can do, what you have done previously, and how you will integrate your products and services into their operation.

Understand what the customer needs—resources, skills, learning, knowledge—and convince them you are the solution.

Good marketing material often works, an easily navigable website is necessary, and clear, effective communication channels are essential.

Think carefully about your potential customers and determine why they will choose you.

27. How will customers find your business?

A big question. If customers can't find your business, you won't have any customers. You certainly won't have enough time to go out and seek each customer individually—some must come to you.

Marketing a service is vastly different from marketing a product. People often need products but might not even realise they need your services—it could be a hard sell.

You will market our business to make it more visible to potential customers and build a database of people you might want to contact in the future. Social media, for example, has completely changed how we interact with the people around us; it allows us to distribute information widely and quickly.

All marketing must be specific to you, it has to be better than the rest, and it must be relevant to the reader.

You can make a good impression on your potential customers using a range of carefully chosen marketing channels.

In all marketing, try to incorporate a call to action and encourage the reader or site visitor to do something, such as sign up for a free whitepaper or newsletter.

Let's have a look at some of those marketing channels which might be used to help your potential customers find your business.

Clearly, you're not going to use all of these ideas—choose the ones you're comfortable with, the ones you have time to do, and the ones you can afford.

- **Brochure**

  Good marketing material is a must. The content must convey:

    o What products or services you can provide, including the products and services you already deliver to other customers. Build on your experience and knowledge.

    o Why you are better than the others offering similar products or services

    o How you will add value to the customer's life or business

  A simple brochure you can send or give your potential customer leaves a lasting impression.

  Get it right; your marketing material is often the key to opening doors.

- **Advertising**

  Advertising is always constrained by budget, but often, there is a strong correlation between advertising spend and the number of enquiries—it's why we advertise.

  Advertising is an investment.

  Let's be realistic; suppose you spend £1000 on advertising and get ten enquiries.

  Firstly, will you be able to service those enquiries efficiently? And, if you do, what if half of those turn into contracts—would you have the capacity?

  Start small and monitor the effect of advertising— determine what works best.

  Your advertising channels must be carefully chosen; where will your advert be seen by your potential customers?

- **Calling**

  Picking up the phone and ringing a potential customer is an art form, especially if you're calling to introduce yourself.

  Do some research to make sure you're speaking to the right person and have a script ready to ask and answer questions.

  Overall, have a clear objective for the call—to secure a face-to-face meeting, perhaps.

  Cold calling is difficult, but it will become easier, more enjoyable, and more productive with some practice.

- **Whitepaper**

  An authoritative whitepaper on a hot topic can be a great way to introduce your business to potential customers.

  As you build your network of potential customers, demonstrate your knowledge by regularly publishing whitepapers.

  You can publish the whitepapers on your website with a link from social media or email.

  In some cases, you might request visitors to leave their name and email address to gain access to the whitepaper.

- **Survey**

  Surveys can be a great way to discover something about your potential customers—their needs, concerns, challenges, etc. Online surveys take no more than a few minutes to create, and some are entirely free.

  Suppose people leave their name and email address in return for a copy of your survey report. In that case, you're on your way to creating a marketing database.

  A well-written survey report can impart helpful knowledge and showcase the solutions you can provide in response to the survey findings.

- **Referral**

  A referral from a customer is a compelling introduction to a potential customer.

  Ask any customers if they're willing to pass your details on to people in their network or whether they could recommend someone you might contact to offer your products or services.

- **Speaking**

  Being on a stage in front of key players in your market or industry is a free advertisement. You have a chance to tell them what you know or how you overcame a challenge they're facing.

  The value of public speaking is immense. Search for speaking opportunities, for example, conferences, forums, seminars, Chambers of Commerce, Meetups, The Rotary Club, and business clubs.

- **Newsletter**

  A small regular newsletter puts your business into the offices of potential customers. Electronic newsletters are relatively easy and quick to create and distribute to thousands of people within minutes. Keep the content topical, current, and entertaining. You must use a dedicated mailshot service. Don't send a mailshot from an email address—it could create SPAM issues, which might block any further attempts to contact the potential customer. More on mailshots later.

- **Book**

  Have you ever thought about writing a book? A book is a brilliant way of showcasing your knowledge; it's captured there within the pages. A 150-page book with illustrations would contain around 30,000 words. Authors such as Michael Crichton aim to write 10,000 words each day. So, he would be writing almost two such books a week. Being realistic, with some planning and plotting, you could write a book within a few months.

  Imagine meeting a potential customer for the first time, taking them through your products and services, and leaving them with your business card, marketing brochure, and a signed copy of your book.

Trust me; the impact is massive.

- **eLearning**

  A small eLearning module—maybe 20 minutes long—would take no more than three or four hours to produce. A snappy title, hot topic, and valuable content could impart helpful information and knowledge to potential customers, and showcase your expertise. Of course, include your business details are highlighted at the end of the module.

- **Podcasts, Webcasts and Webinars**

  Similarly, podcasts, webcasts, and webinars don't require much time and effort to be put together. A snappy title, hot topic, and valuable content could impart helpful information and knowledge to potential customers, and showcase your expertise. Each creates an opportunity for you to introduce your business.

- **Breakfast briefing**

  As you build your network in a specific region, it might be appropriate to invite your network to a breakfast briefing, where a single hot topic is covered by you or another expert.

  Updates to regulations and legislation always make for outstanding hot issues, and often, the body responsible for the new law is happy to provide an authoritative speaker. So, you can give helpful information for minimum outlay and create a chance to meet potential customers face-to-face.

Meetups, for example, are a great way to bring people together, showcase your knowledge, and provide information. Any member of Meetup can start a new group of people in their region with similar interests.

Fortunately, I have a Meetup group in my area that meets just 100 metres from my office.

- **Networking**

Networking is often seen as a trivial activity. Networking is an excellent opportunity to showcase your knowledge, expertise and business. Find and create opportunities to meet with potential customers, people within your market or industry, and people facing the same challenges as you—prepare to distribute many business cards.

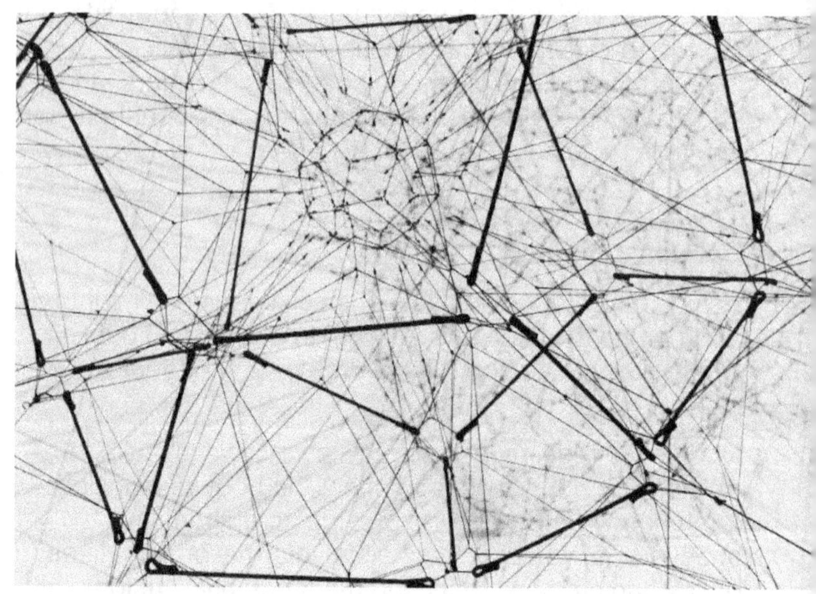

More on networking later.

- **Social media**

  Not all social media is conducive to marketing and business. However, sites such as LinkedIn have a firm grip on millions of like-minded professionals.

  Often an attempt at a direct sell won't be successful, so try to build communities and relationships.

  LinkedIn provides many excellent opportunities to tell people about you and your business. For example, you could start a LinkedIn Group to share and collect thoughts on your chosen topics.

  If you're new to social media, start by watching other people—create a professional presence, don't be too pushy and avoid overloading the site with advertising.

  Use social media wisely; aim to post something weekly, preferably with a good image or video.

  Keep the content relevant to your audience. Starting a discussion can create a following.

- **Website**

  A good website is a great way to showcase your business.

  There are many excellent website-building applications; creating a great impression takes no more than a few hours.

  Look what your competitors are saying—with a bit of imagination, you could do better.

- **Sponsorship**

  Often, by sponsoring a business event, you can connect with local businesses.

  The event doesn't need to be massive; it just needs a small gathering, such as a networking event (a Meetup perhaps), where you could offer breakfast or lunch.

- **Directories**

  Being listed in a directory allows your business to be seen by people searching for products and services.

  There are hundreds of directories on the internet; some of those might apply to your business, and the listings are often free.

  It's worth doing some research to discover the opportunities for directory listings.

- **Google**

  The world's leading search engine offers a host of features you can use to give your business more visibility.

  Use the Search Engine Optimisation function to get your business high on the listings—let your listing be found.

  Spend time understanding what Google offers and making the most of its services.

  Also, take some time to provide the necessary information, such as keywords and tags, to identify your business.

- **Business card**

  A business card is an essential tool for anyone promoting a business.

  The card must be visually pleasing, uncluttered, readable, tactile, informative, and printed on both sides.

  Aim for a standard-size card; too large and it's not going to be filed with other business cards, too small and it'll get lost.

- **Exhibition**

  Visiting trade exhibitions usually costs nothing, but it's a valuable opportunity to talk with other visitors, to get updates on new products and services, and to consider how your business might develop in future.

  Take your business cards.

- **Magazine article**

  Offer to write magazine articles—editors are always looking for great content.

  Research the magazines your potential customers might be reading, approach the publishers to check the main topics in forthcoming issues and start writing the article. Start writing as early as possible to avoid the pressure of publishing deadlines.

- **Press release**

  Use the power of the press to get your message out there. You can submit your news to thousands of news outlets and search engines using a press release distributor.

Writing a press release isn't the same as writing an advertisement or website content. Hit the reader in the first line, tell them your news and why it is crucial (such as benefits to humanity), and include your contact details.

Design a press release template using no more than three or four paragraphs.

Ensure you include a statement from the business owner (you) and maybe a comment from a customer.

Most press releases are limited to fewer than 400 words, so the writing can be a challenge—keep it exciting and on-topic.

- **Email**

Using email to communicate with potential customers might seem an obvious way of advertising your business. It's inexpensive, it's quick, and it's direct. However, before we get too excited, email has its drawbacks.

Deliverability can be an issue; often, bulk email gets tagged as SPAM or simply goes missing—as much as 12% in the UK.

The sheer volume of emails provides a smokescreen; some people receive hundreds of emails daily. Then, the opt-out clause allows people to unsubscribe from your mailing list.

If used correctly, email can quickly build your brand and your business. A great email must be instantly attractive, informative and personal.

Use graphics to grab attention. Ensure the email is responsive and will display correctly on every device— 67% of emails are read on phones.

Include a meaningful Call to Action (CTA), offer the reader something, and, in return, ask them to provide an email address.

If misused, email can be a nightmare. Use email marketing software to provide a professional image and to avoid SPAM filters.

Once your email gets stuck in a SPAM filter, you could be on a slippery slope; such filters tag your mail and prevent it from being delivered now and in the future. Email marketing software costs around £100 annually.

So, how will customers find your business?

28. Does the business already have any customers?

There is a great benefit in having customers lined up before the business is set up.

Firstly, there is the relief that your products, services, skills, knowledge, and experience are saleable. It gives you the confidence and the assurance to press ahead with your plans to be self-employed.

Secondly, you know you will have income.

Thirdly, you know what your customers want from you. So, as you're putting your business plan together, concentrate on what those customers ask you to do and work on those products or services.

29. Describe the marketing strategy for the business.

We have already mentioned that the budget can constrain advertising. Advertising is an investment; when done well, it can pay dividends. Think about your advertising strategy. Will you spend your budget at the beginning of the year or month by month? Will you focus on adverts in magazines, mailshots, or both?

Do some research and look at what your competitors are doing—does it appear to be working?

Above all, please don't put all your marketing efforts into one campaign unless you know it will pay dividends immediately. Use different channels and different approaches.

Consider the best advertising channel and how it might work with your other marketing activity.

30. How will the business attract new customers?

Being realistic, new customers aren't just going to show up with a signed contract.

Describe the entire process from marketing to contracting— what will you do to get the customer onboard?

View your business from the customers' perspective; make it easy for them to understand what you're offering and how they can get more information.

Your contact details should be prominent in every piece of marketing.

31. Describe the competitors.

- **Who are they?**
  Consider the businesses you will be competing with.

- **Where are they?**
  For each competitor, describe where they're based and where they operate.

  If you're unsure, do some market research—don't guess.

- **What do they provide?**
  For each competitor, describe the products or services they provide.

  Do more research.

  What is their USP—is it clear?

  Are the competitors a real threat?

  If so, how can you reduce the risk?

32. Identify the Strengths, Weaknesses, Opportunities, and Threats.

Thinking about you and your business, identify the strengths, weaknesses, opportunities, and threats (SWOT).

> Strengths and weaknesses are internal attributes; opportunities and threats are external.

> Equally, strengths and opportunities are helpful, while weaknesses and threats are harmful.

Go through your business and consider every element of it—it's not easy unless you drill down to minute details and consider every element of it—think about stuff you never even thought about before: your age, for example (are you too old?), your children (do they rely on you for support?), your parents (do they rely on you for support?), your sales and marketing skills (are they excellent?), your IT skills, and so on.

There is no right or wrong way to do this, nor are there any wrong answers.

Take your time to complete the analysis following the SWOT framework example below—this is for a small grocery store.

	STRENGTHS	WEAKNESSES
HELPFUL	Family owned Low salary and benefits Know the market Flat structure—quick decisions Adequate staff coverage Small business Access to cash	Need shop premises No business experience No IT skills School breaks—childcare
	OPPORTUNITIES	THREATS
HARMFUL	Adapt for new markets New university On-campus premises	Uni—summer break Rely on uni to provide custom Needs IT investment

With the completed framework, concentrate on turning weaknesses into strengths over the coming weeks and devising plans to eliminate the threats by converting them into opportunities. SWOT is a great tool for identifying the elements of the business that could be helpful or harmful.

33. Identify the actions to be taken from the SWOT analysis.

What measures must you take to convert the weaknesses to strengths and to eliminate the threats?

The Weaknesses and Threats might make starting a business very difficult. Ensure you fully understand them and are planning actions to eliminate or reduce them.

The identified actions must be specific, with a timescale for completion of each action.

34. Describe the day-to-day operations.

Consider the management tasks—those tasks you don't get paid for but are essential for the business to run, such as.

- Invoicing
- Banking
- VAT
- Bills
- Marketing—website, social media, PR, and communications
- Scheduling
- Contracting
- Product/Service development/improvement
- Customer Relationship Management System
- Networking
- Learning

Running the business can easily consume one day each week; which day will you choose?

HINT. It's not Saturday or Sunday!

Devise a checklist of what you must do that day—maximise your effort and minimise the 'non-earning' time.

Put VAT (if registered), marketing, invoicing (if appropriate) and banking at the top of your list of priorities—have a detailed plan.

Remember to keep your customer records up to date.

There is a complete chapter on running your business later in this book.

35. Describe the operational facilities.

Most of your work will be undertaken in your or the customers' workplaces. I mentioned your place of work when we covered the Business Address.

You might consider other aspects, such as where you will meet new customers, where you will train customers (if needed), etc.

If you're working from home, you might need to consider renting an office by the hour for customer meetings.

36. Describe any contractors or suppliers and how they will be used.

At this point, you must be clear about the support you will require and be sure it's covered in the financial projections.

We're not interested in stationery providers, but you may need to consider an accountant and a solicitor.

Also, consider how you might use other experts to enhance your product range or customer service level.

Again, consider the cost and income, and include them in your financial projections.

37. What equipment does the business need?

- **At Start-up?**

  List the equipment, including processing equipment, you need to operate your business from the startup.

  You might use processing equipment to address your customers' needs.

  Of course, you need a phone, a computer, and a printer.

  But, you might also need ovens, fridges, a cement mixer, a vacuum cleaner, a van, a wetsuit and tanks, a car, a lathe, a tractor, a boat and some nets, a lawn mower, and so on. The list is almost endless.

  Consider renting the necessary kit, if possible, or paying for it in installments.

  With a detailed list, get estimates of cost.

- **In the first year?**

  List any additional equipment you might need within your first year of operation—get cost estimates.

- **In the first three years?**

  Thinking ahead slightly, list the equipment you might need in the next three years that's not already listed.

  Get estimates of cost. Most of the office equipment you will need is electronic—phone, computer, printer, etc.

  These would typically be depreciated over three years or so and possibly replaced at that time.

38. Describe the assets of the business at the Start-up.

List the business assets at the outset besides your electronic office equipment.

Be rigorous—include furniture, lamps, processing equipment, storage—anything that will be used for over one year which is not consumable.

Such assets are called 'capital assets' or 'capital expenditure' for tax purposes.

Assets could include software, especially any software purchased outright and used for over two years.

Itemise any such software, including office, design, and Customer Relationship Management (CRM) software.

39. What materials or stock does the business need?

List the startup materials or stock, which could be anything from nail polish to cows, from food to lengths of timber.

Be specific—exact specifications, potential suppliers, lead times, quantities, and prices.

You also need to think about payment terms, which depends on the types of products/materials being bought and their use. Could you pay for them after you've been paid, or will you dip into the reserves to purchase what you need?

40. Will the business hold patents, trademarks, licences or other proprietary rights?

List the intellectual property, patents, trademarks, and copyrights that could be considered assets.

41. Start-up expenses—describe the required expenditure before becoming operational.

- **Workspace.** All premises-related expenditure.

- **Travel.** If you plan to travel, maybe to meet potential customers, estimate travelling costs.

- **Clothing.** Protective clothing or specified uniform, but not everyday clothing.

- **Staff.** All employment-related costs.

- **Legal and Financial.** All legal and financial costs, including Professional Indemnity Insurance.

- **Marketing.** Make a clear plan, build the plan into your weekly routine, and forecast the monthly cost. We'll look at the details in the next Chapter.

- **Sales.** Estimate the costs, if any, of sales before startup.

- **Other.** Include any pre-operational costs which have not been listed.

Be realistic; expenses and costs will be incurred before start-up. It's essential to understand what those costs will be and consider their impact on your personal finances.

42. Payment policy.

A defined payment policy is essential for sound financial planning; the consistent approach lets you forecast the payments in and out and calculate the balance.

Bills from suppliers. Try to pay bills to a routine. For example, on Friday, immediately before payment is due.

Invoices to customers. Always agree on the payment terms with your customers.

Be sure to invoice customers precisely as agreed and chase any unpaid invoice immediately after payment is due—any allowed slippage will become the norm.

So, if the payment terms are strictly 30 days from the invoice date, call the customer at 09:00 on the 31st day if payment hasn't been made. Speak to the person directly responsible for approving your payment.

Draft an outline policy on payments coming in and going out.

43. Describe the pricing structure and rationale.

Pricing is tricky.

You're not selling a commodity; you're selling yourself, your products and services—what are you worth?

Would a low price bring more business?

One of my former competitors charged half my daily rate; did he get twice as much work?

Think about the value of the products or services you provide, then consider:

> Do you expect to work five days each week?

> Do you expect to have only four weeks of holiday each year?

> Do you expect to pay national insurance contributions (NIC)?

> Do you expect to pay into a pension scheme?

44. Finances

Let's make some assumptions:

> Working three days each week and taking six weeks' holiday each year roughly equals 132 working days/year.

> As a sole trader, let's say you must make £4,800 a month to cover bills, mortgage, living expenses, and your pension.

£4,800 net income monthly equates to around £7,125 gross monthly to you (before tax and NIC deductions).

From the business, £7,125 net out monthly is around £9,000 gross income.

£9,000 monthly is £108,000 yearly, which equals almost £820 per day.

That's your breakeven. 11 days each month, earning £820 each day.

44a. Draft Income Statement—Projected monthly income.

Create a table with 13 columns.

See the example in ANNEX B1.

Label the first column 'ITEMS', this is where you can list your chargeable services or products.

The other 12 columns will be identified as the months of the year, but since we don't know our start date, we can label them 1 to 12.

In these columns, you can insert the potential realistic monthly revenue for the first year.

By adding up each column you will determine your potential monthly income.

44b. Financial Year End Date (Month/Day).

As a sole trader, the financial year-end date might align with the tax year.

For a limited company, the year-end date is decided at the time of incorporation.

44c. Business start date.

As a sole trader, the business start date is the date at which you registered as self-employed.

For a limited company, the business start date is the date of incorporation.

44d. Draft Expenditure Statement—Projected monthly outgoings.

Create a table with 13 columns.

See the example in ANNEX B2.

Label the first column 'EXPENSES', this is where you can list your expenses under the headings of Wages, Premises, Materials, Travel, Communications, Marketing, Materials, Utilities, Legal, Accountant, etc.

The other 12 columns will be identified as the months of the year, but since we don't know our start date, we can label them 1 to 12. In these columns, you can insert the anticipated monthly expenses for the first year.

By adding up each column you will determine your potential monthly expenses.

By adding a row to capture the Gross Profit from 44a, it's now possible to calculate the projected net profit (Gross Profit minus Total Expenses).

45. What to do BEFORE the business can start operating, and how long each activity might take.

Your business plan is almost complete. You need to take some time to familiarise yourself with the content, ensuring that you know what it all means.

As we leave the planning stage behind, we head into the setting up phase—that's assuming all the financial calculations show that the business is viable.

If you've followed this book page by page, a lot of the setting up process is just that; setting up.

Many of the decisions have already been considered, researched, and possibly decided.

Based on the business plan, I've prepared a checklist of the end of the planning stage and the start of the setting up stage.

The purpose of the checklist is to ensure the setting up gets done, hopefully in the right order, and to highlight that the setting up is not going to happen overnight—there's still a lot of work to complete—and that's the exciting part; it's your business.

1. Decide on the company name
2. Determine the type of business
3. Assess business bank account options
4. Calculate the financials
5. Finalise the business plan, including the timetable
6. Make the big decision to go self-employed
7. Get an accountant
8. Secure a business address
9. Register with Companies House
10. Open a business bank account
11. Start financial records
12. Get a mobile phone
13. Get a workspace
14. Get equipment
15. Assess all opportunities for marketing
16. Get domain name

17. Design a logo
18. Determine website/marketing keywords
19. Plan website/marketing structure and content
20. Secure email addresses
21. Develop a website
22. Develop a social media presence
23. Research potential customers
24. Develop a simple CRM system
25. Contact potential customers
26. Get Insurance
27. Register as self-employed
28. Register for VAT
29. GO Self-Employed!

Use the list to create a plan that will lead to completion of the setting up phase by estimating how long it might take to complete each activity.

The list can also be used as a checklist to monitor progress.

Decision Time

OK, you've now got enough information to help you make the decision on whether you go self-employed.

No one can decide for you, but you might ask family, friends, and maybe colleagues for their advice.

To help with your decision-making, let's take a look at the mathematics; in your business plan, you included a number in response to the question 'How much money do you NEED to earn monthly?'

In your business plan, you projected the monthly income, expenditure, and net profit; so calculate the expected revenue (net profit) for the entire year.

- **Sole Trader:**

  As a sole trader, your net profit is classed as gross income and is subject to tax.

  Determine your personal allowances, tax rate, and national insurance contributions.

  Calculate your net income (Gross income minus tax and NIC).

- **Limited Company:**

  As a limited company, your net profit goes to the business and is subject to corporation tax.

  You will draw a salary from the business.

  Determine your personal allowances, tax rate, and National Insurance Contributions from your projected salary.

  Calculate your net income.

Calculations

Does your projected net income show that the business will cover your financial needs (NEED to earn)?

If not, you must increase your projected income, reduce your forecast expenditure, or both. Don't forget to factor in any funding or other sources of income.

If the numbers don't stack up, revisit them, check them—
maximise the income opportunities and minimise the
expenditure (without cutting corners). Ask yourself whether
you need an office or need to travel business class.

Also, look at the cash flow and calculate how much you must
pay out before you start earning any income—where will the
money come from?

When the figures stack up, you can make the big decision.
But, as you know, it's not just about the money. Think about
the effect on your family and your lifestyle.

I'm focussing on data protection,
especially the new regulation.

FOUR:
SETTING UP YOUR BUSINESS

Getting started

In this chapter, there will be some duplication from previous Chapters—we will cover similar topics but from a different perspective; we were planning, and now we're setting up.

These are exciting times; you need to spend the next few weeks transforming your business plan into an operational business. Some work will be challenging, but every step brings you closer to being self-employed.

Realistically, your business plan is good, but it still needs much work before the income starts rolling in. Using the timetable you created at the end of the business plan, we will establish your new business step by step.

Elevator Pitch

But, before you begin the exciting journey to getting your business up and running, I must mention your pitch, sometimes referred-to as the elevator pitch.

Your pitch should be a brief phrase that tells everyone what your business is about; it's your mini advertisement.

A great elevator pitch is short, informative and includes the USP. It's best to develop your pitch so it can be used to explain your business to everyone you're going to meet over the next few weeks—accountant, bank manager, suppliers, potential customers, etc.

It's worth spending some time polishing your pitch to make it stand out, and then practice saying it. Tell everyone about your business in a snappy, exciting sentence.

- **Scenario One [you are Alan]**

  'Hey Alan.'

  You instantly recognise the voice, and as you turn, you see the familiar smiling face of an ex-boss Ben heading towards you.

  'Hi Ben, it's good to see you; it must be what, three years? How is Jerry, and what about the twins—they must be all grown up?'

  'They're good, thanks for asking. I heard you're going to set up your own business; sounds exciting.'

  'Well,' you reply, 'it's . . . er . . . just a consultancy business . . . working from home—you know the sort of thing.'

  'OK,' says Ben, 'good luck with that—sorry, I have to dash. Have a good weekend. It's great to see you.'

- **Scenario Two [again, you are Alan]**

  'Hey Alan.'

  You instantly recognise the voice, and as you turn, you see the familiar smiling face of an ex-boss Ben heading towards you.

  'Hi Ben, it's good to see you; it must be what, three years? How is Jerry, and what about the twins—they must be all grown up?'

'They're good, thanks for asking. I heard you're going to set up your own business; sounds exciting.'

'That's right,' you reply, 'I'm focussing on data protection, especially the new regulation.'

'Wow, you were always good at that,' says Ben, 'in fact, you might be able to help us; the new regulations are causing us a few headaches. Do you have a few minutes—let's grab a coffee?'

In the second scenario, just nine words—the pitch—made a massive difference to the conversation.

'I'm focussing on data protection, especially the new regulation.'

Ben was told everything about the business to the extent that he could decide if he needed those services. The clever part of this pitch is it also defines the problem (new regulations). Focusing on the regulations infers an ability to solve some of the issues—that's the USP.

What's your USP? Think about it, make a note of it, and then simplify it repeatedly. Polish those words until they're perfect, and they just trip off the tongue.

Get an accountant

Accountants are vital figures in any organisation; they provide valuable services and knowledge to help the business run smoothly and profitably.

For limited companies, your accountant can offer support during the start-up phase, such as getting your business incorporated with Companies House, for example, and providing advice on record keeping, etc.

When the business is established, your accountant will prepare your statutory accounts for submission to Companies House along with your Confirmation Statement, and assist with tax calculations and wages, for example.

If you are a Director of a Limited Company, for example, you will draw a salary requiring a payroll with tax and NIC deductions.

Your accountant will arrange for the required payments.

Typically, for a limited company, an accountant could offer:

- Financial advice
- Online accounting service
- Annual Statutory Accounts (Prep and file)
- Annual Corporation Tax Return (Prep and file)
- Director's payroll (Prep)
- Annual Confirmation Statement (Prep and file)
- Director's Personal Tax Return (Prep and file)
- Quarterly VAT Return (Prep and file)
- Registered Office
- Business Incorporation (Prep and file)
- Invoicing
- Reporting
- Annual General Meeting (If required)

The costs for providing such services vary significantly but shouldn't be more than £250 per month*.

Obviously, the services a sole trader requires are not so exhaustive and should cost less than £60 per month*.

(At the time of writing*)

Secure a business address

Many options for your business address vary depending on whether you are a sole trader or a limited company.

- **Sole trader**

  The easiest and cheapest solution is to use your home address, which is perfect if you work from home. If you decide to rent premises, you might use that address. I choose to work from home where possible and use a virtual office as a postal address. The virtual office also provides a meeting room and desk space—paid hourly—should I need it. Such flexibility costs a few pounds per month and is my ideal solution.

- **Limited Company/Limited Partnership**

  Limited Companies need a Registered Office. If possible, the easiest and cheapest solution is to use your accountant's office as your Registered Office. Otherwise, use a virtual business address or virtual office as a Registered Office. When searching for a virtual business address, shop around. You may see the same addresses being used by several providers; merely find the cheapest; prices vary considerably.

I choose to have my business address in London, close to a train station. That way, I can call in to collect my mail anytime I'm in town.

I could choose to have the letters sent to me, but I found the cost of such a service prohibitive. Interestingly, I found several providers offering this essential service for free in a recent search for a virtual office.

Obviously, the costs mount should you choose additional services—mail forwarding, call answering, etc.

Registering with Companies House

All limited companies must register with Companies House—this is known as incorporation. Your accountant should provide all the support you need, but for guidance, we'll walk through the stages together.

Before you start to incorporate, you need:

- A suitable company name, which is in the Business Plan.
- A Registered Address for the business.
- The name/s of the Director/s.
- Details of the shares—price and number of shares. Your accountant will advise. Most companies fix the price at £1 per share and have 1000 shares—there are no rules.
- Your SIC code (Standard Industrial Classification) to identify what the company does.

The five-digit code explains your business activities. The Companies House website, and others, have an extensive list—select the code corresponding to your business.

You might choose, for example, SIC Code 95250. Repair of watches, clocks, and jewellery.

- A written agreement to form a company, signed by each of the Directors, even if there is only one Director.

  This document is called the Memorandum of Association. A template can be downloaded from the Companies House website.

- A document defining the rules under which the company will operate—known as the Articles of Association.

  Model articles can be downloaded from the Companies House website; these must be reviewed thoroughly to ensure they're adequate for your business.

- Details of People of Significant Control over your company.

  You are required to identify and list those people in your company who have significant control. Significant control is defined by three general rules.

  - Someone who holds more than 25% of the shares
  - Someone who holds over 25% of the voting rights
  - Someone with the power to appoint or remove the majority of the Directors.

Suppose your company is limited by shares and adopts the model articles of association. In that case, you can register your company online at the Companies House website. It costs £12, and it takes no more than 24 hours.

However, you may need to modify the articles. In that case, you must register your business by post using form IN01, available from the Companies House website. Registering by post costs £40, which takes around eight to ten days.

Open a business bank account

We've already assessed the various business bank account options and shopped around for the best deal. Before you open the account, I urge you to make one last check—is it the best deal, and is the account the most suitable for your company?

Over the past 20 years, I've opened several new business bank accounts, and I find it increasingly easier.

The last account I opened took me no more than three or four minutes to apply online, and I had the account confirmed within the hour. The account suits me perfectly since all my banking is online, reducing fees considerably. The account also allows me to specify my virtual office address as the business address. All correspondence is sent to my home. This also reduces the virtual office cost since they're not handling any postage from the bank.

Start financial records

From the outset, you must record all expenditure and income. Several methods can be used to capture the transactions efficiently.

Your accountant will advise you on the most suitable way for your company, which will capture the information your accountant needs to create your financial reports.

At a basic level, each transaction should be captured in a record that contains:

- The date of the transaction
- A description of the transaction
- Whether the transaction was a receipt or a payment
- The balance
- An explanation of the transaction, e.g. stationery, transport, rent, mobile phone, wage, etc.

Using accounting software is the easiest and most effective method of capturing each transaction; again, your accountant will advise. Get into the habit of keeping records and maintaining your accounts frequently.

Get a mobile phone

I've included a section on getting a mobile phone because, in my experience, it can be tricky, if not impossible, to get a mobile phone for a business. Phone companies appear to be making it difficult for companies to open business accounts and buy mobile phones.

The last time I tried to purchase a mobile phone for a business, I wanted one phone—which seemed to upset the phone suppliers I spoke to; they were looking for a much larger contract.

The business was a limited company (limited by guarantee); the phone company requested details of all the directors, including their residential addresses; they wanted to do a credit check on each. Phone companies must do a credit check before any contract can be agreed upon. It often requires them to check each of the directors. One director refused to provide those details, so I didn't buy the phone.

Suppose there is only one company director (you). In that case, the process will be much simpler, but be aware of the necessary checks.

One solution is to buy the phone personally and charge it to the company—your accountant will advise the best way of accounting for a mobile phone.

Get a workspace

We briefly looked at the location of the business in the Business Plan. We considered working from home or rented premises depending on your business needs.

Generally, working from home has advantages, such as:

- It's inexpensive compared to renting an office or workspace

- It's convenient and avoids the long commute
- You control the working environment
- You have more time for you
- Some might argue that there are fewer distractions from people working around you, making you more productive.

It all sounds good, except when working from home, you might discover.

- You're working in solitary confinement—it's just you
- You're working longer hours
- Someone keeps moving your stuff
- Actually, there are more distractions, and you're less productive

Working from home makes it more difficult to switch off at the end of the day, especially when using the dining room as a workspace. Your business can gradually impact the entire family, and your family can affect your business. You might find, over time, you're taking the kids to school, collecting the dry cleaning, picking up the groceries, etc.

Getting rented premises isn't always going to solve all your problems. OK, you might avoid the domestic distractions, but there is the expense of renting the space, and there's still the commute.

For me, the ideal solution is to create a dedicated working space at home. When I started-out, I worked in my newly renovated garage; it was perfect. I went to work at the same time every morning and tried to finish at the same time every afternoon.

Even though I was only three metres from home, I avoided using the house during the day (except for comfort breaks).

Everything I needed was in the office.

Your workspace must have adequate lighting, heating and ventilation, sufficient power points, and internet access.

When working from home, the most crucial factor is being able to close the door on the work at the end of the day.

Get equipment

Depending on the type of business you're setting up, you will need the tools of the trade—ladders, mowers, ovens, a van, etc.

You will need a desk, filing, storage, a computer or a laptop; you also need a desk chair that is supportive, adjustable and comfortable.

Then, there's the software and a printer; choose the printer to suit all your anticipated needs—paper sizes, colours, double-sided, photo quality, Wi-Fi, etc.

Office equipment is classed as capital. Keep receipts for all your purchases.

Although not strictly equipment, the software is also classed as capital if purchased outright and intended to be used for over two years.

If you decide to go VAT-registered, you can reclaim the VAT you paid to purchase the equipment.

Even if you're not VAT-registered, keep the receipts; you have up to four years to reclaim the VAT.

Assess all opportunities for marketing

In the last Chapter, when completing the business plan, we listed various methods, from advertising to exhibiting, under the question 'How will the customers find your business?'.

It's time to revisit the list and decide what methods you will use to help your customers find your business.

Advertising	Book	Breakfast briefing
Brochure	Business card	Calling
Directories	eLearning	Email
Exhibition	Google	Magazine article
Networking	Newsletter	Podcasts
Press release	Referral	Social media
Speaking	Sponsorship	Survey
Webcasts/Webinars	Website	Whitepaper

The best way to start thinking about your marketing is to develop a marketing plan; a good plan will describe how you will deliver your marketing strategy—your plan will become a reality.

A coherent marketing plan will help you decide which customers, markets, and industries to approach, how to contact them, how to win their business, and how to build a profitable relationship.

We will work together on each of the seven steps of the marketing plan.

A formatted copy of the marketing plan can be downloaded from the publisher's website:

https://www.pen-2-paper.co.uk/downloads.html.

So, let's start by outlining your marketing strategy.

- **What is your vision?**

    The vision is in your business plan.

- **What are your objectives?**

  The objectives are in your business plan.

- **How will you achieve those objectives?**

  By describing how you will achieve your objectives, you will define which customers and markets you should approach and how you might communicate with them.

  I can't stress enough the importance of identifying potential customers and designing your approach to suit their needs.

  Consider. do all your potential customers have the same needs, or must you have more than one approach?

- **List the different needs of your potential customers.**

  By segmenting your potential customers according to their needs, you can address those needs by matching them to your strengths. Your marketing objectives should align with, and support, your business objectives.

  For example, one of your business objectives is to generate £80,000 gross revenue in the first year.

  Another objective might be to develop an auditing service specifically for charities.

  So, one marketing objective might be to approach the charities that are reporting growth and may need an auditor. All your marketing objectives should be clearly defined with timescales for completion.

  Next, consider the tactics you must adopt to win business, such as how you will describe your products or services to your potential customers.

Also, at this stage, the most efficient marketing methods and the frequency of each method must be determined.

We mentioned earlier the scale of any marketing activity. the levels of effort and investment in marketing. I always treat marketing as a journey, taking one step at a time, following the plan, and doing what works.

Start small, building your business one customer at a time, and monitor the marketing successes to understand the best marketing channels.

In many respects, your marketing plan will be similar to your business plan. We're not going to reproduce your business plan here.

Still, I suggest you refer to your business plan as you develop your marketing plan.

Your marketing plan is a living document; you should review and change it as your business develops and grows.

- **For each of your products or services, identify their features, benefits, and proportion of sales revenue.**

  Create a four-column table. Label the columns Products/Services, Features, Benefits, % of Sales.

  See the example in ANNEX B3.

  In the first column insert one of the products/services you will provide—let's say, Management Systems Auditing.

  In the next column insert the main feature of the product/service; we're saying that the audit is multi-faceted—it covers more than one management system standard.

Insert the benefits of the multi-faceted audit in the next column—from the customers' perspective. Let's say it is more comprehensive and it delves deeper into the systems. It's going to be more cost-effective and less intrusive.

By completing this simple exercise, you will have identified the benefits of your products or services from the customer's perspective; the benefits will be your USP. Some people struggle to recognise the benefits of their deliverables.

Possibly, the best way of identifying the benefits is to interrogate the features by asking SO WHAT?

In our example, the management systems audit is multi-faceted and not just based on one management system audit standard—SO WHAT?

By being multi-faceted, the audit is more comprehensive. It delves deeper to identify potential weaknesses and non-conformities. Plus, there are cost-savings to be made. Those are the benefits.

Next, you must identify the types of businesses you will sell to. Consider their needs versus the benefits of your products/services.

- **For each customer type, identify their needs and compare each need to a benefit.**

Create a three-column table. Label the columns Customer Type, Needs, and Benefits.

See the example in ANNEX B4.

The purpose of this table is to identify how your products/services satisfy the customer needs—to ensure that you can provide what they need. As an example, let's consider a small but growing charity; the benefits of a multi-faceted audit are immense. But, perhaps they don't know that—maybe they have different providers for each type of audit.

So, we have to understand the needs of the customers versus the benefits of what you provide—sell the benefits.

We're starting to build a clear picture of your potential customers; we know the types of customers, what they need, and how your product or service will satisfy their needs.

You now need to consider communicating with each customer type—what media will you use?

Then consider what your message might say, how much effort the marketing requires, and at what cost.

- **For each message type, identify the methods of communication, the time of the first message, the required effort, and the likely cost.**

Marketing often comprises two very basic messages:

- This is who I am/we are.
- This is what I/we do.

For each, consider the most appropriate methods of communication.

If you're in front of a customer, an audience, or an individual at an event, it's all about you and your business. In those circumstances, the communications have to be on-point. You are the USP.

So, to communicate who you are, use Business Cards, Speaking Opportunities, Podcasts (speaking to a wider audience), and Social Media.

To communicate what you do, use Advertising, Websites, Brochures, Surveys (and survey reports), Webcasts, and Webinars.

Consider when any of these methods might be used:

- During the business start-up
- Periodically, after the start-up (State the frequency)
- Daily (for social media)

For each of the methods consider the time and the cost. For example, a daily social media post (or repost) takes only a few minutes and costs nothing. Whereas advertising, through Google, might cost £100/month.

See the example in ANNEX B5.

Which is more effective?

As you complete this exercise to understand what methods could used and what might be most effective, notice how the different communication methods impact the time and cost.

Social media might consume 120 hours of your time each year (around 30 minutes each day), and your survey might take 50 hours yearly. But which is most beneficial?

While running your business, the total marketing effort in this example is 333 hours each year. Be realistic and prioritise the marketing effort; do only what is necessary. Consider the value of the survey or social media. Aim to accomplish between four and six hours of marketing each week.

It would help if you determined how potential customers will contact you through each channel. Use various means to point prospective customers toward your business and to you, such as email, phone, or online enquiry forms.

So, when it's been filled in, your marketing plan is completed.

Four tasks in the marketing plan must be completed before the business starts operating—designing your brochure, building your website, setting up email, and creating your business card.

You must also finish some 'enabling' work in preparation for these tasks.

Get a domain name

We covered your domain name briefly as we completed your business plan. You checked the domain name's availability and decided what Top Level Domain (TLD) to use.

Your chosen domain name pinpoints your website's location on the World Wide Web. Your domain name supports your brand and business.

Besides the TLDs, there are country code domains such as .uk, and hundreds of generic top-level domains (gTLDs) like .net, .org, .london, .eu, etc., to be considered.

The geographical implications might be important, as they can affect search results.

When registering your domain name, your provider will charge a small fee to protect your name throughout the period of registration.

It is important to note that you can't buy the domain name outright—the fee covers the name for the registration period only and is usually recharged annually.

We haven't covered website hosting—because we don't yet have a website. However, website hosting packages often include domain name registration.

In fact, we haven't yet decided how to build the website; some website design platforms provide hosting, domain names and emails—a one-stop-shop.

Based on your website design skills and budget restrictions, there are many ways you could build your website—you could do it yourself, use site-building tools, or hire a web designer to make it for you.

In any event, I believe it's essential for you to understand how to design, develop, and maintain your website.

Building the website yourself requires knowledge of coding, especially HTML or CSS, and website-building software.

The many excellent site-building tools allow you to build your website quickly and relatively easily. Select a theme for your site, customise your site, and add apps to improve functionality.

Site-building tools are available from web hosting companies and usually involve a monthly or annual payment.

Hiring a web designer is not an overly expensive option, but it can be the most difficult depending on the size and complexity of your website—how will you tell the designer what you want? Defining a clear design brief can be daunting.

Be aware of the General Data Protection Regulations (GDPR) requirements and your site's privacy notice, terms and conditions, etc. Also, be mindful of accessibility issues; ensure your site is available and visible to all users.

I use one of the many site-building tools; there are many to choose from, such as Wix, Squarespace, Site123, 1&1 IONOS, web.com, Weebly, Bookmark, Jimdo, etc. Some of these sites are free to use.

Weebly is my choice, but I haven't used all the others. A simple, three-page website can be built within a few minutes if the words and pictures are available beforehand.

Be careful when selecting the site builder option—know precisely what you're paying for. You need a website, a website host, a domain name, and, possibly, an email address—all linked and working.

Weebly does everything I need; it's quick, easy and inexpensive.

Design a logo

Logo design requires a measured approach based on psychology—understanding what makes your potential customers tick, what emotions a logo can provoke, and how people behave according to their perceptions.

People often think designing a logo is easy. They mainly focus on the colours or the font they will use. Unfortunately, there's much more to the psychology of logo design. Any logo directly relates to the brand's image; it's your company's visual representation that potential customers will recognise and connect to.

It's important to understand that every element in your logo will have a psychological effect, whether it is your intention or not.

The term logo comes from the Greek logos, which means 'word.'

So, when you design a logo, you create a visual word to convey a message to your potential customers and make them relate to it. As they relate to words, they'll do the same with your logo from their unique perspectives.

Different shapes affect people differently; certain geometrical objects have particular meanings.

Your choice of the shapes in your logo will convey a specific message to your potential customers.

For example, circles often represent community, family, or femininity; triangles are often associated with law, power, and even masculinity; rectangles tend to express logic, rationality, etc.

Before choosing a shape, research what it might represent and what kind of message it conveys. For example, if your products are focused on men, go for an inverted triangle.

The psychology of colour states every hue can have a variety of meanings.

The psychology behind colour is complicated, but you need to understand that colours can invoke certain emotions and ideas:

- Yellow, energy, youthfulness, happiness—friendly and playful.

- Red, anger, passion, excitement—confident and fearless.
- Green, conservation, nature, life—sympathetic and caring.
- Blue, calming, assuring—professional and trusting.
- Purple, luxurious, fascinating—mysterious or diverse.
- Black, luxurious—minimalist and modern.
- White, clean, uncluttered—minimalist and youthful.

Like shape and colour, font selection can enhance a logo. Four kinds of font are used to create a unique logo that conveys the right message:

- Serif fonts, classic, sophisticated, elegant, vintage, old-fashioned.
- Script fonts, handwritten, calligraphic, sophisticated, playful.
- Sans serif fonts, simple, uncluttered, clean, modern.
- Display fonts, decorative, stylised, attention-seeking.

By combining different fonts, the typography can create a great-looking logo. But don't go too far and make your logo a mishmash of styles. A font should be instantly readable.

Determine website/marketing keywords

Computer search engines use keywords to locate what people are looking for. The technology behind search engines is highly complex; the number of daily searches runs into billions.

Conducting keyword research is crucial to getting the right keywords into your marketing. Start by considering your landing page—the first page your site visitors will see—and decide the main keywords.

Consider the search terms your customers might use to find your product or service. Develop a mixture of short keywords like 'watch repairer' and long-tail keywords like 'watch and clock repairer'. Try to include variations of words, such as watch, watches, clock, clocks, timepiece, timepieces, etc.

You might also consider keyword-matching options:

- **Broad match**—If your keyword is 'watch repairer', with broad match, a user who types in either 'watch' or 'repairer' in any order, with any other words, may find your site.

  The broad match might deliver many impressions, but the results will be irrelevant, leading to poor sales.

- **Phrase match**—With phrase match, your site will only show if the search term contains the exact keyword, amongst other words.

  Phrase match is more targeted than Broad Match and should generate higher sales.

- **Exact match**—With exact match, your site will only show if the search term contains the exact keyword with no other words.

  Exact match is very targeted but could result in few people finding your site.

The keywords you use in the website content should be the same as your printed content and vice versa.

Don't create two sets of marketing—website and printed—avoid telling two different stories or creating two distinct impressions.

Plan website/marketing structure

A good website or brochure won't automatically lead to a successful business.

To be beneficial, your marketing must be accessible, simple to use/read, and relevant to potential customers.

Before you start the design of your website and brochure, you must consider the following:

- purpose—what do you want your website and brochure to accomplish?
- users—what devices will be used to access your site, and how people will obtain your brochure.
- structure—the order of pages and how different pages should be laid out.
- design—how the website and brochure will look and how the site might be used.
- content—the information you want to publish, using the keywords.

Let's talk about your website first.

A layout with a straightforward page arrangement is critical to the function and appeal of your website.

An excellent design will help users quickly navigate the site and find what they want.

Poor layout leads to poor user experience and may deter customers from accessing your products or services.

Wireframing allows you to create a site mock-up and show the primary sections. The design elements should include only the main layout, the website structure, and the organisation of pages (the framework), not the words and graphics. The wireframe might comprise boxes with labels showing their contents and the links between those boxes.

I use yellow paper squares (Sticky Notes) for my wireframes.

Wireframes should be clear and easy to understand. They can be created by hand or by using office software.

Owing to their simplicity, wireframes are easy to alter. They're handy for showing the navigation around the site.

Your brochure should echo the main elements of the website—maintain the look and feel.

Use the same text and graphics when building the site and your brochure.

Draft website/marketing content

Your marketing content should be relevant, helpful, and appealing to attract potential customers. The material doesn't need to sell your products or services directly, but it does need to build a relationship with the reader.

Good content allows you to grow your brand awareness and increase the number of business contacts, helping you develop your audience, understand your potential customers, and meet their needs.

Relevant, helpful and appealing content gives your readers a reason to delve deeper into your website or brochure. The ultimate aim is to convert readers into customers. Over time, you will notice what readers are interested in, which helps you develop future content.

Quality content is essential. Great content invites people to read more and look at what you do. The same material can be used across all marketing activities, such as advertising (PPC), social media, and SEO.

However, writing good content can be challenging, especially coming up with good ideas and finding the time to write them.

Start by setting objectives—what do you want to achieve from your marketing? You might want to build your brand awareness, generate sales, or drive traffic to the critical parts of your website. Consider who you are trying to attract. Research their interests and create content that will speak to them directly. Using social media, look at what has attracted the most attention in the past. Research the topics and the delivery formats—discover what works the best.

Create content to attract an audience; it should be incredibly enlightening, enjoyable, relevant and original. Make your headlines stand out; grab the audience's attention by using strong keywords—display powerful graphics, such as infographics, photos, graphs and even videos.

Always look for a fresh angle, a way of telling a story or presenting information in a unique way.

Put a new perspective on known facts, introduce a new way of thinking, or start a discussion—be controversial but supportive of your readers' viewpoint.

Write your content, review it, edit it, study it, revise it, and go back and polish it—make it shine. Please don't stop until you're entirely sure it's perfect. Then, at the same time, think about graphics, colours and fonts.

I always collate the website graphics before I start to build the site; it saves time later and allows me to concentrate on developing the website instead of finding pictures, writing content, etc.

Use your words, graphics, fonts, and colours across all marketing platforms, linking to the website wherever possible.

Try to create a look and feel that, in time, will be recognised as your brand.

Carry the brand on every marketing piece, including your business card, emails and invoices.

Secure email addresses and set up emails

Email addresses should match your domain name, so if your domain is qwertyuiop.com, your email address should be set up at anthony@qwertyuiop.com, info@qwertyuiop.com, or something similar.

At all costs, ensure there is a clear divide between your personal email addresses and your business email address. Avoid email addresses that are accessible by members of your family or give the appearance of not being totally secure, for example, anthony@wilkinsonfamily.com.

Also, ensure your email is coming directly to you, not someone else. Companies are reluctant to send confidential documents to an email address that is slightly dubious.

Companies and email software will often have issues with email addresses such as Hotmail, Gmail, Mail, Yahoo, and other domains, which can appear as spam. Many domain name providers and web hosts offer an email service as a package.

These bundled services are often cost-effective, and easy to set up and maintain.

Email marketing

Marketing by email can be an efficient and influential approach to potential customers.

Email marketing allows you to send tailored messages to your potential customers based on customer preferences.

Email marketing also allows you to respond to customer actions as a result of your email by, for example, offering incentives to complete a transaction within a defined timeframe.

By monitoring your email marketing campaigns, you can measure how each message is performing, which can gauge the effectiveness of your approach. Those changes might relate to the timing of your emails, the use of graphics in your emails, and the words used in your messages.

Marketing your products or services by email can be a quick and cost-effective way to reach potential customers. It allows you to create bespoke messages, which often improve response rates.

However, marketing emails can irritate people if their content is inappropriate, too regular, or unwelcome.

Email marketing is scalable and can be scattered to many potential customers or targeted at a select few.

Direct email marketing must comply with the Privacy and Electronic Communications Regulations (PECR). The regulations require you to, for example, identify yourself and offer an email address. You might need to consider email marketing list opt-ins and opt-outs, which means you can email an individual only if they consent. Opt-in requirements don't apply to email marketing between companies. However, by sending an email to a company, you don't know who will read it.

The General Data Protection Regulation (GDPR) introduced new rules for processing and safeguarding personal data.

Breaches of the GDPR may attract fines of up to 4% of your business's annual turnover. The unsubscribe option allows an individual to unsubscribe from your email marketing by a simple link in your message. The law says individuals must be allowed to unsubscribe from email marketing.

As you build a customer database, you can segment your email marketing list with their details, responsibilities, interests, and preferences.

Segmentation allows you to target your products or services only to relevant groups. Suddenly, your message is more relevant to the receiver. Relevance leads to more clicks and, hopefully, more sales.

If, for example, you're selling IT equipment, aim your messages at the IT guys.

Unsolicited email messages are illegal. People need to sign up for your email marketing list. They're more likely to do that if you offer them an incentive, for example, special discounts on selected products/services. This approach is beneficial when offers are available only through your email marketing channel.

Good email practice (GEP)

Consider your target audience, what you're trying to achieve, and how you might measure success.

Prepare your email processes.

The quality of your email marketing list is more important than quantity. To maximise the quality, cleanse your marketing lists regularly.

Your email message must be accepted by Gmail, Hotmail and Yahoo Mail. Check the spam score for each email campaign.

Most email software will scan your email before sending it, giving your message a spam rating and highlighting issues for rectification.

The email's subject line will often dictate your message's open rate. The subject line is your shop window, which entices the potential customer. An engaging subject line will encourage them to click on your email,

Send your emails at a time when potential customers are most likely to open them.

All customers are unique, so do your research and test the audience to measure and understand the best time and day to send your emails.

To make your email marketing successful, it must be tested, analysed, adjusted, retested, etc. However, modify and check only one element at a time so you know what part made the difference.

Monitor the effectiveness of your emails to be sure you're making the most of your time and effort.

Most email service providers offer data tracking:

- Delivery success, including details of bounces
- Opens and open rate
- Clicks and click-through rate
- Unsubscribes

Email software can be set up to send emails automatically to a website user based on their actions.

Email marketing essentials

People choose to read an email by looking at the subject line. The subject line must be short—50 characters. Use keywords and generate a sense of urgency.

Email marketing tells people things they're interested in— keep it simple and focused.

Segment your marketing lists so people only receive relevant emails.

Identify what the customer should do when they open your email. Place your call-to-action in a prominent position.

Give people the option to stop receiving your email. Use an 'unsubscribe' option on every message.

Measure the effectiveness of email campaigns to determine what works and what doesn't. Test and analyse to improve clicks and sales.

Email software

Email software is used to create, send, receive and organise your email. It provides advanced features for managing email, including editors for composing messages, security protection to prevent spam and phishing, and advanced test capabilities to ensure your email isn't going to get stuck in your potential customers' email filters.

Some great packages are available to make your emailing campaigns easy and effective. All the leading providers can send automated emails triggered by an event on your website, manage your mailing lists, including unsubscribes and undeliverables, and provide detailed reports from the campaign. MailChimp and HubSpot are possibly the market leaders; each offers scalable solutions to match your business needs.

Develop a website

If you've followed this book page-by-page, you should have a website designer (or site builder software if you're going to do it yourself), a website host, a domain name, and an email address—all linked and working.

We will build the website using your keywords, structure, and content. All the planning and preparation allow you to concentrate on the look and feel of the site instead of what to write and what graphics to use. I will assume you're creating the page yourself using site builder software.

A user-friendly design plays a starring role in the presentation of your site. Exceptional design allows you to meet the needs of your website visitors by creating an excellent experience.

User-friendliness comes from the functions and features of your website that make it easy to use, for example:

- Online or live help
- Navigational aids
- Visual prompts

Your website visitors must be able to find information quickly and easily. Otherwise, they get bored or frustrated and go looking elsewhere.

There are three essential elements you need to consider:

- What do your visitors expect to do on your website?
- How might your visitors want to interact with your website?
- How might you make it easy for visitors to find what they need?

Standardise the look and feel of each page, and keep the navigation elements in the same place. Make it easy for the visitor to get to the right place—follow the three-click rule where the visitor can go from the landing page to the required information (and a call-for-action) within three clicks. This requires intuitive navigation and great use of keywords.

Avoid putting too much content on a page; it will appear cluttered and disorganised, which might prevent visitors from finding the information they need. The clever use of links can divide content between different pages. Still, the visitor should know how to find it intuitively, making the navigation seamless.

Place all essential elements so they're visible as the page loads. Don't expect visitors to scroll around the screen looking for the buttons you want them to press.

Let's focus on building your pages; using the wireframes you created earlier, create page templates to define a familiar layout across the website.

Such consistency provides smooth transitions between pages.

Place vital elements in the same position on each page, especially menus and navigation bars, buttons, etc.

Use the same fonts and colours throughout. The choice of font is essential; use a standard font to avoid being replaced by a default system font that won't look right.

Make your page hierarchy clear.

Display your logo in the same place on each page. Link the logo to your homepage.

Display your search box in the same place on each page.

With your wireframes in place, fill the frames with graphics and content. Work on your homepage first, loading the frames until there is enough content and graphics.

When you're happy with the homepage, move on to the next page.

All the time, focussing on the navigation, aim for a smooth transition between web pages. Building your website might take a few hours; don't rush; get it right.

Now, you need to test your webpage across all platforms and on all types of devices—make sure it works on each. Over 50% of email is read on a mobile device; if your potential customer clicks the link to your website from their phone, they expect to see your site correctly rendered.

So, you've now got yourself a website—well done! Unfortunately, having a great website is only part of the story; how will anyone find it?

Of course, the answer is people will search using a search engine, and the search terms will match the website's keywords. However, it's not that simple.

Firstly, keyword searching for a watch repairer on the internet returns over 1.3 million results. Secondly, how will the search engine find your keywords?

Using a search engine optimisation (SEO) strategy, you can get your website listed so it appears higher in the results list—you don't want to be at the bottom of a list of 1.3 million watch repairers. I won't get into the details of SEO, mainly because search engines constantly evolve. What works today might not work in a few months or weeks. Also, I don't know what site builder software you've used.

In your site builder software, look for the section relating to SEO. Add your keywords to your site's SEO section and each page. That approach will get your pages found, but maybe not highly ranked. To help the search engines understand your website, label each graphic with an appropriate name—don't use 'picture 1', 'picture 2', etc. Try to use keywords in your labels.

Next, go to Google Analytics (GA) and create an account. Google Analytics is possibly the most powerful web analytics tool available—and it's free. GA will help you optimise your website to make it more visible. It will also monitor and measure site visits—by language, country, city, gender, age, and operating system (desktop and mobile). GA also counts page views, the number of visitors, when they visited, etc.

It's worth spending some time understanding how GA works—it will make a massive difference in your understanding of your potential customer behaviour. Using Google Analytics, you can test the effectiveness of your marketing campaigns and begin to understand what works.

Develop a social media presence

Social media can be a great way to network, advertise, impress, learn, share, give, etc. You can grow your audience across social media platforms for a few minutes daily. Your social media audience becomes your marketing list.

The right choice of social media platform is essential.

You might already have a personal presence on some popular sites, and you could be familiar with how they work.

Consider how each social media site could support your business from the outset.

The top sites for personal and commercial use are:

- Facebook is the number one site for networking and sharing; it can be used in business.
- Instagram is mainly a photo-sharing site with a limited business application.
- YouTube is a video-sharing site with great appeal—you need some good video content to post.
- X allows message and picture sharing and resharing, which is good for business.
- LinkedIn is the number one site for business, allowing users to build business pages, join groups, etc.
- Pinterest is mainly an artistic photo-sharing site with a limited business application.
- Reddit is a news-sharing site mainly populated by individuals. Readers rate each post.
- Tumblr is a microblogging site mainly aimed at individuals.
- Flickr is a photo-sharing site with a limited business application.

Social media allows you to showcase yourself and your business and share some of your knowledge with like-minded professionals, including potential customers.

But social media can be highly time-consuming, so you need a plan of what content you will post, where you will publish, and when.

It would help if you also decided where the content will come from; you can't afford the time to write a whitepaper or article each day.

So, let's start with the basics. where and when will you post?

I might suggest developing a LinkedIn personal page, a LinkedIn company page, a Facebook company page (separated from your own personal page), and a Twitter company page (separated from your personal page).

As a product/service provider, separating your LinkedIn pages will be challenging since people will want to know who you are.

So, it's a good idea to have personal and company pages on LinkedIn, make them visible, and promote both.

We now know where to post but don't know when to post.

I suggest you develop a simple plan for posting content, for example.

- LinkedIn personal page   Monday
- LinkedIn company page   Tuesday, Thursday
- Facebook company page   Wednesday, and Friday
- X company page   Daily

Next, you need to decide what you're going to post. Think about the content people will want to read—here's the surprise, it won't be what you expect.

In my experience, people speed-read through social media, only clicking on immediately appealing content. They don't search for the material; they read or mostly ignore what's in front of them.

Every social media post needs a tremendous graphic or video because it requires no reading or interpretation. Equally, the post's title must instantly appeal, encouraging people to read on.

The entire social media post should be no more than 40 words, with a link to more content—possibly on your website, with a call to action.

That's just three clicks from your social media post onto your marketing list via your website, meaning your site must be continuously updated with hot content—perhaps once a week.

I think you will be hard-pushed to create brilliant content for your four social media channels. However, you don't need to make the content; re-post something already out there but repackage it.

I'm not talking about plagiarism; I'm talking about posting a famous quote, re-posting a highly relevant news article, or publishing some fascinating statistics as an infographic. Boost credibility by naming the source of the material or even connecting to the source.

With X, you need to decide what you will post daily—mostly, you will be retweeting posts from other people, but with your own spin. X is mainly used to keep up with the latest news; the only way that can happen is by passing the story on to the next person. Occasionally, you must post something original on X—take something from your other social media channels.

Some excellent software packages can help with content creation, marketing and distribution. Curata and Feedly, for example, scour the web seeking interesting content. Both packages learn what works best and continuously evolve to help you create great social media posts every time. Hootsuite allows you to schedule and distribute content across many channels. So, you can make the content for LinkedIn and Facebook on Monday morning and let Hootsuite do the rest.

Finally, let's talk briefly about YouTube. A video is a powerful marketing tool, but it must be developed and delivered professionally for it to be helpful in a B2B environment. It takes time, and it needs a compelling story.

Start by looking at YouTube videos from other professionals in your market or industry; what are they talking about? If you have an exciting story, try speaking with a video camera on your smartphone.

Be honest; is it compelling? Also, when looking at the videos from other professionals, notice the number of views and consider whether your video will be seen by enough of the right people.

Research potential customers

So far, in setting up your business, we've mainly concentrated on how your customers might find you. Your company will be exposed to your future customers by marketing and advertising across different channels.

Now, we will switch the focus and look at how you might find those elusive customers without waiting for them to come to you. And, here's the best bit, we will use all the methods we already covered—social media, websites, and so on—not yours, but theirs. We're going to research your potential customers; then, you're going to contact them.

Before we do any of that, let's think about the reality. It doesn't matter how amazing you might be; your potential customers aren't interested—they want someone to solve a problem.

Unfortunately, in many cases, they don't realise they have a problem. So, you often try to sell them something they don't know they need.

The only way you're going to convince a customer they need your products or services is to FULLY understand the challenges they're facing. The more you know their business, the more of an expert you will appear to be.

Use social media to understand what your potential customers are interested in. A simple Facebook or LinkedIn company page or group will hopefully attract potential customers—find out what groups they belong to, what they're posting, and what they're sharing. On LinkedIn, conduct a search using a job title and see who pops up.

Spy on your competitors by looking at what they're doing—don't just copy it; make it better for you. Google can make your task easier by setting up a Google Alert for a specific term and seeing what people seek. Search your competitors' social media and websites to understand what they're doing.

As you're gathering data on potential customers, you need to store the information in a manner that provides easy analysis and access.

Develop a simple CRM system

A good Customer Relationship Management (CRM) system can help you track and manage communications with potential and current customers.

The information captured in a CRM system might include customer details, contact details, sales history, communication history, and the analysis of the marketing efforts. Additionally, CRM systems can often automate customers' communication, which helps provide a consistent and wholesome customer experience.

The main benefits of a CRM system stem from the accessibility of the information on any device at any time. One dedicated system in a cloud stores all the customer-related information; no more spreadsheets, emails, and lists containing customer information—it's all there in one place.

Many CRM systems are large, complex and expensive. As a product or service provider with many customers, you need something that's easy to maintain yet still provides functionality.

Research the multitude of available CRM systems, and choose one that suits your needs and your budget; don't ignore free solutions such as HubSpot CRM.

Any CRM system is only as good as the information contained within it. It would help if you committed to updating the information—more on that later.

When you've decided what CRM system to use, learn how to set it up using dummy information.

Practice inputting your dummy data, learn how to manipulate and analyse the data, and gain experience in how you will use CRM to drive your marketing.

Once you're confident you know what you're doing, delete the dummy data and start to input the findings from your customer research—you're almost ready to go live with your business.

Contact potential customers

This is it. You're about to contact your potential customers and get your first order or assignment.

Please return to your business plan and merely follow it; complete all the tasks scheduled during the start-up phase. Ensure you've got all your marketing material and content because now is the time to implement it.

Using your CRM system and your contact database, approach each potential customer in the most appropriate manner. Always include a call to action in your message and promise to give them something in return.

Then, within a few days of the initial contact, follow up with a similar message but using a different method of communication.

Check your social media and website analytics, and discover what people have found interesting.

Get Insurance

While insurance isn't compulsory in most industry sectors, inadequate insurance coverage can be a risk.

Professional Indemnity (PI) insurance provides protection if something goes wrong.

PI Insurance can easily be purchased online and should cost no more than a few pounds per month, depending on the level of coverage.

Register as self-employed and Register for VAT

Registering as self-employed is often quick and easy. Registration involves creating a Government Gateway account. It's usually possible to register online, and it takes no more than a few minutes.

The registration process asks the site visitor to confirm, 'I want to tell HMRC that I am in business and need to register for a new tax or tell HMRC that the company is now active'.

Value Added Tax (VAT) is a tax charged on most goods and services provided in the UK. The VAT is also charged on some products and services from overseas. VAT can only be charged by a VAT-registered company—known as a 'taxable person' (someone who is registered for VAT).

The current VAT threshold is £85,000; any company with income more than the threshold must register for VAT. Some companies, especially those dealing with business customers, might feel the advantage of being VAT-registered and can register voluntarily.

In some cases, being VAT-registered boosts a business profile by creating an impression that the company is more significant than it actually is. Also, some larger companies avoid dealing with companies that can't produce a VAT invoice. Being VAT-registered can ease your business dealings.

All VAT-registered companies must file a VAT return every three months. The VAT Return shows the value of sales, the VAT charged to customers, and the value of purchases and the VAT paid.

Registering for VAT is quick and easy. Registration involves creating a Government Gateway account. It's usually possible to register online, and it takes no more than a few minutes.

FIVE:
RUNNING YOUR BUSINESS

Before you start

Again, in this Chapter, there will be some duplication from previous Chapters—we will cover similar topics but from a different perspective; we were planning and setting up, and now we're beginning to run the business.

We're finally at the point where you're ready to go. In reality, the point is not so clearly defined; you may find you've already picked up some work from previous customers, or word-of-mouth has worked in your favour.

Before you start, there are a few things you must consider.

If you're running your business from home, you might need permission from your landlord or mortgage provider.

You might also need to tell your home contents insurer, as your current policy might not cover your business.

You might need to tell your insurer and the car lease company if you use the family car for business.

You are responsible for your own health and safety. Acquaint yourself with Health and Safety laws and get guidance on your responsibilities, if any.

You're also responsible for Data Protection. Get up to speed with GDPR law, etc., and learn about your responsibilities.

The Advertising Standards Authority (ASA) independently regulates all advertising in the UK. Be aware of their codes and how they might influence your advertising, especially online and using your website and social media. The ASA will prosecute any offenders. All marketing should be decent, legal, honest and truthful; it must not mislead.

It's time to start running your business.

Doing the business AND running the business

At the start of this book, I explained the two most critical elements of being self-employed; DOING the business and RUNNING the business.

To recap, doing the business is what you do for customers and get paid for, whereas running the business is managing your business, such as marketing, sales, business development, monitoring, reporting, invoicing, banking, purchasing, record keeping, etc.

As we were developing the business plan, I suggested you put aside one day each week to run your business and devise a task checklist to complete that day. To help, I've devised the following list:

- VAT
- Invoicing
- Banking
- Bills
- Maintaining records
- Customer Relationship Management System
- Marketing and Communications
- Scheduling
- Contracting
- Product/Service development/improvement
- Networking
- Learning

Let's have a quick look at each.

VAT

Some people struggle to get to grips with VAT; I often find the best way to understand VAT is to consider you're collecting the tax from your customers on behalf of the tax authorities and claiming back the VAT you paid to your suppliers.

The VAT Return should be completed and filed online every three months, and it takes only a few minutes to complete if you've got all the information to hand.

By updating your VAT records weekly, the quarterly return becomes a breeze.

Invoicing

I have strict rules about invoicing, which, I believe, allow me to be paid on time.

Firstly, be sure to invoice the customer precisely as agreed.

Secondly, chase any unpaid invoice immediately after payment is due; otherwise, slippage will become the norm. So, if the payment terms are strictly 30 days from the invoice date, call the customer at 09:00 on the 31st day if payment hasn't been made.

Thirdly, and most importantly, ensure the invoice is accurate—don't give the customer an excuse for not paying.

Remember, your company details should be on each invoice. As a sole trader, that should include your name. You should include the company name and company number as a limited company. Here's a list of everything your invoice should include.

- A clear title—INVOICE
- A unique invoice identification number
- The name and address of the company being invoiced

- The date of the invoice
- A clear description of the products or services provided (the items)
- The number of units per item provided, the rate per unit, and the total per item (without VAT)
- Your business name and, for a limited company, the company number
- Your business address and, for a limited company, the registered office address if different
- If VAT registered, your VAT registration number
- If VAT registered, the percentage VAT applicable to each item, the amount of VAT payable for each item, and the total amount for each item, including VAT
- The total amount due
- The invoice payment due date

Banking

As an advisor, for example, you will mainly be paid by bank transfer. If your invoices are due for payment, check daily to see if the transaction has been made.

Anyone dealing with the public is probably going to be dealing with some cash. Make sure the money is banked regularly—ideally, every night.

Keep your financial records up to date, and cross-check with bank statements to see that everything is in order. Retain copies of all correspondence, including statements, from your bank. You should know the status and contents of your bank account every day.

Bills

For payments to suppliers, make the payments as agreed. Check the supplier invoices as they arrive and make any necessary queries immediately. Please don't wait until it's time to pay before noticing an anomaly.

Encourage your suppliers to accept online payments by bank transfer or debit card.

Keep your financial records current, and cross-check with bank statements to see that everything is in order. Retain copies of all bills and receipts.

Maintain records

The law says you must keep all records associated with your business.

Here's a breakdown of the documents you are expected to maintain:

- All amounts paid into the company and their origin—refer to your invoice number if applicable
- For all amounts paid out of the company, refer to the supplier's invoice number, if appropriate, or to an order number.
- All amounts taken from the business as a wage
- Business mileage
- Minutes of Board Meetings, if applicable
- Bank statements

Create the record as close to the transaction or event as possible; keep the records for seven years.

Documents don't need to be held as paper; they can be electronic as long as all the information is captured and is recoverable.

Just as crucial to your business are your customer records (potential and actual customers); you need to maintain a database of all your potential customers and record all communication with them. We'll cover customer records next.

Customer Relationship Management (CRM) System

You must update your CRM system weekly or more frequently if possible. All existing customer records should capture all recent activity. Records of customers should record all communication. Contact lists should be expanded to record the details of the people you've met recently.

Be disciplined with your data; ensure accuracy, avoid duplication, and don't file junk data to boost your lists.

Marketing and Communications

Initiating and maintaining contact with existing and potential customers is vital for the success of your business. Accordingly, marketing and communication will consume most of your time running your business.

Emails must be answered promptly, so it's best to check several times throughout the day and respond as soon as possible. Email marketing should be sent weekly—this requires forethought and planning. Don't send emails that won't encourage a response—clarify the message.

Likewise, check your social media channels throughout the day, responding to posts as soon as possible. Again, you should regularly send social media marketing with a strong message—possibly the same message you used in your email marketing.

Please spend some time with Google Analytics every week, looking at who's visited your website and what they looked at. Based on your analysis, go to your site and make any necessary adjustments to enhance the visitor experience and encourage them to take action.

At the same time, make sure the information on your website is up to date and relevant—'Latest News' shouldn't be more than two weeks old.

Call potential customers regularly, build a rapport, arrange to meet them, understand their challenges and offer viable solutions.

Advertising should be addressed weekly, even if you're not advertising each week. Seek opportunities for advertising and design your advert accordingly.

Aim to advertise monthly. Similarly, through the press, messages are spread to a broader network.

Create interesting opportunities and stories to pique interest in your work, such as publishing a white paper, a webcast or a podcast on a controversial topic.

Broadcast the new item widely using all marketing channels.

Once or twice a year, offer to speak at a meeting or conference. Get in front of an audience and dazzle it with your knowledge, understanding and command of a relevant topic.

Design an annual survey that draws an audience by participating and then by wanting the results. An excellent study can be a helpful marketing tool.

Scheduling

I've stressed the importance of doing the business and running the business.

Running the business often requires essential tasks to be completed within an established timeframe—VAT returns, tax returns, and confirmation statements.

Likewise, from a financial perspective, customers must be invoiced, and payments must be collected.

To ensure you don't miss any important dates, it's a good idea to create a schedule.

- Keep one day free each week to run the business (not Sunday).
- Capture important filing dates—VAT, tax, etc.
- Include essential exhibitions and conferences.
- Clearly mark your holidays.

With a detailed schedule, you can call customers and set dates for meetings, working days, and so on without fear of your plans clashing with other activities.

My schedule is up to 18 months in advance; I update it constantly and reprint it weekly.

My schedule is also accessible on my phone.

Contracting

Before you begin any work with a new customer, you must agree to the terms and conditions of your engagement.

A written contract between the two parties (you and the customer) should be accepted and signed by both. By signing the agreement, each party agrees to meet the other party's demands.

You must ensure that your requirements, such as the payment of invoices, are included in the agreement and not just those requirements specified by the customer.

A typical contract for the provision of products/services would include.

- The name and address of the customer
- The name and address of the supplier (you)
- Definitions of keywords and expressions used within the contract, such as IPR, GDPR, VAT, etc.
- Terms of the engagement, including a statement that you're not an employee, partner, or customer agent.

The terms might also include a comment about your tax liabilities not being covered by the customer.

- Products or services to be provided, including any identification and rectification of poor workmanship.
- Non-exclusivity of the contract, allowing you to work for other customers at the same time.
- Fees to be paid, including how and when. The requirement for invoices needs to be covered in this section—be clear about where the invoice should be delivered and the name of the person responsible for payment.
- Also, if your fee is a daily fee, be specific about part-days, overtime working, weekend working, and travelling, for example. If your customer requires you to drive for two hours to another site for a meeting, you must agree to the payment terms for your travel time.
- Expenses, and what (if anything) you can claim for, such as travel, subsistence, etc.
- Insurance and indemnity, including providing professional indemnity insurance coverage to an agreed limit. Depending on the nature of the work, some companies also specify the need for public liability insurance.
- Intellectual Property Rights arising from the engagement. The customer will specify that the IP belongs to the company, not you, the supplier.
- Confidentiality and the protection of information, including the return or destruction of information at the end of the contract.
- Guarantees include the right to work in the UK, conflicts of interest, etc.
- Data protection and compliance with applicable laws.
- Termination and the customer's right to terminate the contract.

- Notices relating to the contract and how they will be given.
- General Contract conditions.

If you have any doubt about any element of the contract, seek clarification from the customer. If the matter cannot be resolved, seek professional advice.

Take your time to fully understand the agreement, and don't sign a contract you don't understand or disagree with.

Product/Service development/improvement

Advances in technology, changes to regulation, and improvements in good working practices drive the evolution of everything around you.

Often, working as a service provider, for example, with, say, four or five regular customers, you can get complacent about what's happening around you—you're focused on serving your customers. But, your service must improve continually, not just your technical ability to do the work but your business management too. You've got to be better than your competitors.

Of course, new competitors will constantly emerge, and existing competitors will develop and deliver new products and services innovatively. You must stay ahead of the competition by developing and improving your products and services. Take time to research what your competitors are doing. Understand any emerging regulations and keep abreast of technology.

The COVID-19 pandemic forced organisations to adjust their operations to suit evolving regulations relating to working from home. Online collaboration platforms and the meteoric rise in online video meetings have changed how we work forever.

Self-employed people must embrace technology and be prepared to adopt any products, services, software, platforms or applications that the customer uses . . . or needs.

Remote work has transformed the role of service providers, and many now work from home—no long commutes, more engagement time, a larger region of operation, zero travel costs, etc.

Making product developments or improvements doesn't just require a creative mind; it often needs investment. Where will the money come from? Will the investment put the business, family, or lifestyle at risk?

It's often easier to do nothing—just carry on. But then we might miss a golden opportunity. So, try to maintain a proactive approach to product and service development and improvement; ask customers for feedback, collate a register of complaints, and benchmark your product or service against your competitors.

Networking

Networking is a lot tougher than people sometimes think. However, it can be a significant investment, and it can support your business by introducing new customers. Unfortunately, networking is never a priority. So, you've had a hard day, and there's a Meetup at 19:00. Don't think about missing the meeting; you must maintain contact with your existing contacts and look for ways of increasing your network.

I often find new ways to meet interesting people, such as giving talks at Rotary Club meetings, taking short courses, attending exhibitions, etc.

When I say short courses, I don't mean cookery classes; I mean business improvement courses attended by like-minded professionals.

Networking is a skill; you must practice making it work for you:

- **Purpose**—Don't just collect business cards; have a goal of meeting people who can support you.
- **Converse**—Break the ice by asking people why they're at the event. They could be there for the same reason you are.
- **Connect**—Keep in touch with your contacts outside the networking event. They, too, might be seeking support.

Consider networking as a long-term investment.

You won't attend a networking event and come away with a large contract. Use the network to become known, exchange ideas, open doors, boost your self-esteem, and learn.

You're not alone if you find it challenging to meet new people. Look for others who appear to be slightly uncomfortable and talk to them. Nothing terrible will happen; you'll be surprised by what you can learn from others.

Networking provides an opportunity to learn about potential new customers and assignments. A close network might also offer access to expertise to support your work with your customers. Use your network to increase the scope of your operation; likewise, encourage your close network to do the same.

Learning

Never stop learning; being self-employed, your customers often expect you to know more than they do, so they pay you for your knowledge.

Keep current with applicable regulations, technology, best practices, trends, and insider knowledge. Find great news sources relevant to your market or industry, spend time sifting through them, and retain the critical bits.

Learn new things; the internet provides a vast resource full of great learning opportunities. As soon as you stop learning, you will lose your competitive edge. Below is a list of online learning sources—the list is not exhaustive:

- TED
- FutureLearn
- LYNDA
- Alison
- CodeAcademy
- Khan Academy
- LearnVest
- Hubspot Academy
- Udemy
- Moz
- OpenCulture
- BusinessBalls
- edX
- Coursera

Put aside a couple of hours each week for personal development.

Above all, enjoy being Self-Employed!

BE SO GOOD
THEY CAN'T
IGNORE YOU

ANNEX A

CODE OF CONDUCT

CODE OF CONDUCT

Competence and Behaviour

I avoid situations where my judgment may be compromised or where conflicts of interest could occur.

I maintain professional competence through the continuing development of my knowledge and skills.

I apply high standards of accuracy, relevance and timeliness to advice or information provided.

I understand my professional limitations and will seek support where necessary.

I accept responsibility for their own advice, actions and decisions.

Integrity

I develop and maintain professional relationships based on trust and respect.

I promote equality, diversity, dignity and inclusion, and observe human rights.

I am sensitive to the customs, practices, cultures, and beliefs of others.

I protect confidential information and avoid using it for personal gain.

I am responsible, accurate, honest, and objective at all times.

I abide by the applicable laws.

Professionalism

I understand, promote and implement the applicable laws, regulations, guidelines and standards.

I am aware of the difference between personal preference and professional independence.

I avoid acting on behalf of the customer unless specifically authorised to do so.

I maintain the highest standards of ethical conduct.

I uphold professional duties to society.

Governance

I promote ethical standards and challenge others suspected of unlawful or unethical conduct.

I put my customers' reputations and best interests before my personal interests.

I treat people reasonably and fairly.

Promotion

I support and promote the values and reputation of the profession.

ANNEX B
EXAMPLES

EXAMPLES

B1: Projected Monthly Income (£1000)

ITEM	1	2	3	4	5	6	7	8	9	10	11	12
Auditing	1	2	2	2	1	2	2	1	2	3	1	3
Consulting	2	2	2	2	4	3	2	3	2	4	2	4
Training	1	1	1	1	1	2	2	1	3	2	3	1
Assessing			1		2	1	2	2	2	1	2	1
GROSS PROFIT	4	5	6	5	8	8	8	7	9	10	8	9

B2: Projected Monthly Outgoings

EXPENSES	1	2	3	4	5	6	7	8	9	10	11	12
Wages	2	2	2	2	2	2	3	3	3	3	3	3
Premises	0	0	0	0	0	0	0	0	0	0	0	0
Materials	0	0	0	0	0	0	0	0	0	0	0	0
Travel	0	0	0	0	0	1	0	0	0	0	0	1
Communications	0	0	0	0	0	0	0	0	0	0	0	0
Utilities	0	0	0	0	0	0	0	0	0	0	0	0
Legal	2	0	0	0	0	0	0	0	0	0	0	0
Accountant	1	0	0	1	0	0	1	0	0	1	0	0
Marketing	1	0	1	0	1	0	1	0	1	0	1	0
TOTAL	6	2	3	3	3	3	5	3	4	4	4	4
GROSS PROFIT	4	5	6	5	8	8	8	7	9	10	8	9
NET PROFIT	-2	3	3	2	5	5	3	4	5	6	4	5

B3: Features and Benefits

PRODUCT/SERVICE	FEATURES	KEY BENEFITS	% OF SALES
Management Systems Auditing	Multi-faceted	More comprehensive Cost effective	25%
Consulting	Multi-faceted	Wider scope Cost effective	35%
Training	Multi-faceted	Wider scope Cost effective	25%
Assessing	Multi-faceted	Wider scope Cost effective	15%

B4: Needs versus Benefits

CUSTOMER TYPE	NEEDS	KEY BENEFITS
Growing charity	Compliance Audit	More comprehensive Cost effective
Small manufacturer	Quality and Safety Training Quality and Safety Consulting	Wider scope Cost effective
Not-for-profit	Compliance Audit Training Consulting	More comprehensive Wider scope Cost effective
School	Compliance Audit Compliance Training Compliance Consulting	More comprehensive Wider scope Cost effective

B5: Communication Methods

MESSAGE	METHOD	WHEN	EFFORT (Hrs)	COST (£)
This is who I am/we are	Business Card	Start-up	4	20
	Social media	Daily	0.5/day	0
	Podcasts	Quarterly	2/quarter	0
	Speaking	Yearly	10/year	0
This is what I/we do	Brochure	Start-up	20	200
	Website	Start-up	20	100/year
	Email	Start-up	10	100/year
	Calling	Monthly	4/month	0
	Advertising	Monthly	4/month	100/month
	Whitepaper	2 x Yearly	30/year	0
	Survey	Yearly	50/year	0
	Webinar	Yearly	15/year	120/year

ANNEX C
TERMINOLOGY

TERMINOLOGY

Accountant: An accountant provides the expertise, measurement, disclosure, or assurance about financial information that helps business owners make decisions about allocating resources.

Advertising: Advertising is a form of marketing communication used to encourage a potential or new customer to take action. The most common desired result is to drive them to purchase a product or service.

Articles of Association: Articles of Association are the internal rule book that every Limited Company must have and work by. It sets out the rights and duties of directors individually and in meetings.

Specific statutory clauses must be included; the other clauses are chosen by the members to make up the organisation's bylaws.

The Articles have to be filed with Companies House, who also needs to approve any changes.

Asset: An asset is anything of material value or usefulness that is owned by a person or company.

Bank account: A bank account is a financial account between a bank and a customer. A bank account can be a deposit account, a credit card, or any other type of account offered by a bank.

The financial transactions on a bank account are reported to the customer on a bank statement.

Bill: A bill is an account of goods sold, services rendered, or work done, with the price or charge; a statement of a creditor's claim, in gross or by items. A bill is usually presented for payment.

Breakfast briefing: Breakfast Briefings are usually a panel session of one to two hours. The briefings provide an opportunity for guests to hear from an expert panel on a topic area before moving on to a Q&A discussion for sharing ideas and best practice.

Brochure: Brochures are advertising pieces mainly used to introduce a company and inform potential customers about products and/or services. Brochures are distributed by mail, handed personally or placed in brochure racks.

Brochures are often printed using four colour process on thick gloss paper to give an initial impression of quality. Businesses may turn out small quantities of brochures on a computer printer or on a digital printer, but offset printing turns out higher quantities for less cost.

Business address: A business address is an address at which the business can be contacted. The business address can be the business's physical location; it can be a Registered Office or a virtual office.

Business card: Business cards are cards bearing business information about a company or individual. They are shared during formal introductions as a convenience and a memory aid. A business card typically includes the giver's name, company affiliation and contact information such as an address, telephone number, e-mail address and website.

Business partnership: A partnership is an arrangement where parties, known as partners, agree to cooperate to advance their mutual interests.

The partners in a partnership may be individuals or businesses who may partner together to increase their likelihood of achieving their mission and amplify their reach.

Business Plan: A business plan is a formal statement of a set of business goals and the plan for reaching those goals.

Code of Conduct: A Code of Conduct is a set of conventional principles and expectations that are considered binding on any member of a particular group or community.

Communication: Communication is the activity of conveying information by speech, visuals, signals, writing, or behaviour. It is the meaningful exchange of information between two or more people or between a business and a potential customer. The communication process is complete once the receiver has understood the message of the sender.

Companies House: Companies House is the United Kingdom Registrar of Companies. All registered limited companies, including subsidiary, small and inactive companies, must file annual financial statements in addition to yearly company returns, which become public records.

Company Tax Return: All limited companies must complete a Company Tax Return. The return must be sent to Her Majesty's Revenue and Customs (HMRC) within the correct period.

Competitor: A competitor is a person or organisation who wants access to the customers of another person or organisation.

Confirmation Statement: A Confirmation Statement ensures the public record at Companies House is correct; it needs to be filed annually.

Consulting: Consulting is defined as the practise of providing a third party with expertise on a matter in exchange for a fee. The service can involve either advisory or implementation services. For the consultant, taking an independent and unbiased stance on an issue is central to their role.

Consumable: A consumable is any product or equipment used to conduct and deliver products and services consumed, for example, printer ink.

Contract: A contract is an agreement entered into voluntarily by two or more parties, each of whom intends to create one or more legal obligations between them. The critical elements of a contract are 'offer' and 'acceptance'.

Customer Relationship Management: Customer Relationship Management (CRM) is a system that companies use to manage customer interactions and potential customers. CRM helps organisations streamline processes, build customer relationships, boost income, improve customer service, and increase profitability.

Customer: A customer is the recipient of goods, services, products, or ideas obtained from a seller for a monetary or other valuable consideration.

Director: A Director is a member of a business who may or may not have an executive function. The Director is usually chosen or appointed to control or govern the affairs of a business.

Directory: A directory is a list of names, addresses etc., of specific classes of people or organisations, often in alphabetical order.

Domain name: Domain names are easy-to-remember words that we can use to communicate to a DNS server the website we want to visit. The Domain Name System (DNS) is what translates the friendly name to an IP address.

eLearning: eLearning is training provided via a computer or other digital device, allowing technology to facilitate learning anytime, anywhere.

Elevator Pitch: An elevator pitch is a short summary used to quickly and simply define a product, service, or organisation, and its value proposition. The term comes from a scenario of an accidental meeting with someone important in an elevator. If the conversation is interesting, it will continue after the elevator ride and may lead to new business.

Email: Electronic mail is a method of exchanging digital messages from an author to one or more recipients. Today's email systems are based on a store-and-forward model.

Email servers accept, forward, deliver, and store messages.

Email address: An email address identifies an email box to which email messages are delivered.

Financial records: Financial records are formal documents presenting the transactions of a business. Financial records maintained by most businesses include a statement of retained earnings and cash flow, income statements and the company's balance sheet and tax returns.

Google: Google Inc. is an American multinational corporation specialising in Internet-related services and products. The products and services include search, cloud computing, software and online advertising technologies.

Incorporation: Incorporation is the process by which a new or existing business registers as a limited company. A company is a legal entity with a separate identity from those who own or run it. The vast majority of companies are limited liability companies where the liability of the members is limited by shares or guarantee.

Insurance: Insurance helps business owners protect themselves, employees, customers, and visitors, against risks like fire, accident, theft, illness, or death.

Invoice: An invoice is a commercial document issued by a seller to a buyer, indicating the products, quantities, and agreed prices for products or services the seller has provided the buyer.

Laptop: A laptop computer is a personal computer generally smaller than a briefcase that can easily be transported and conveniently used in temporary spaces. Laptop computers generally cost more than desktop computers with the same capabilities because they are more challenging to design and manufacture.

A laptop can effectively be turned into a desktop computer with a docking station.

Limited company: A limited company is a type of business structure that has been incorporated at Companies House as a legal 'person'.

It is entirely separate from its owners; it can enter into contracts in its own name and is responsible for its own actions, finances and liabilities.

LinkedIn: LinkedIn is a social networking website for people in professional occupations. LinkedIn reports more than 225 million acquired users in more than 200 countries and territories.

Logo: A logo is a graphic mark or emblem commonly used by organisations to promote instant public recognition. Logos are either purely graphic or are composed of the name of the organisation.

Mailshot: Mailshots are bulk mail advertising sent through the mail to potential customers to advertise products or services.

Marketing: Marketing is the process of communicating the value of a product or service to customers to sell the product or service. It is a critical business function for attracting customers.

Marketing plan: A marketing plan may be the part of an overall business plan which describes the marketing strategy and the plans for its achievement, including the costs and benefits of marketing.

Memorandum of Association: The Memorandum of Association is a document that regulates a company's external activities and must be drawn up on forming a registered or incorporated company. As the company's charter, it forms the company's constitution.

Objective: An objective is one of the primary goals intended to be attained by the business.

Office equipment: Office equipment includes desks, chairs, computers, and light fixtures.

Passive income: Passive income is an income regularly received, with little effort required to maintain it. Passive income mainly comes from investments, interest, book sales, rental activity, or earnings for online adverts.

Patent: A patent is a set of exclusive rights granted by a sovereign state to an inventor or their assignee for a limited period in exchange for the public disclosure of the invention. An invention is a solution to a specific technological problem and may be a product or a process.

PC: A PC (or personal computer) is a small digital computer based on a microprocessor and designed to be used by one person at a time.

PSC (Person with Significant Control): A PSC has the right to exert significant influence or control over the business and management of a limited company or LLP.

Personal Tax Return: Self-assessment is used to collect tax from the self-employed, paying income tax on their profits. It is also used if you're a business partner or a director of a limited company.

PI Insurance: Professional Indemnity insurance—also known as PI Insurance or PII—is intended to protect professionals and their businesses in the event of claims made by a customer (or third party) suggesting that they have suffered loss as a result of non-performance, breach of contract and/or professional negligence in the products or services provided.

Press release: A press release is a written or recorded communication directed at members of the news media to announce something ostensibly newsworthy. Typically, they are e-mailed to assignment editors at newspapers, magazines, radio stations, television stations, or television networks.

Processing Equipment: Processing equipment is the kit, machinery, apparatus, you need to do your job—other than a phone and computer equipment.

Process equipment might include a lawnmower (for a gardener), a tractor (for a farmer), an oven (for a baker), and so on.

Registered Office: A registered office is the official address of an incorporated company, association or any other legal entity.

A registered physical office address is required for incorporated organisations to receive official correspondence and formal notices from government departments, investors, banks, shareholders and the general public.

Secondary income: A form of income to supplement the regular (primary) income. When going self-employed, a second income from another job can reduce the risk of having no income.

Self-assessment: Self-Assessment is short for the 'Self-Assessment tax return', a form that many business owners need to send to HMRC each year to report how much they have earned and from what sources. The term 'Self-Assessment' actually refers to the fact it's the individual's—or company's—responsibility to work out how much tax he or she should pay. The Self-Assessment tax return is usually just called a tax return.

Self-employed: A self-employed individual works for themselves rather than for a specific employer. A self-employed individual earns income by contracting with a business directly. Someone who is self-employed will receive payment with no tax withholding in many cases; thus, they are responsible for paying their taxes correctly.

SIC code: The Standard Industrial Classification (SIC) is a system for classifying industries by a four-digit code. Established in the United States in 1937, it is used by government agencies to classify industry areas. The SIC system is used by Companies House.

Social media: Social media refers to interactions among people in which they create, share, and exchange information and ideas in virtual communities and networks.

Sole trader: A sole trader—also known as a sole proprietorship—is a simple business arrangement whereby one individual runs and owns the entire business. Sole traders are legally responsible for all aspects of their business and are personally liable for their business's finances. While they can keep any profits, they may also have to repay any debts out of their own pocket.

Solicitor: A solicitor deals with any legal matter and should be consulted over issues such as contracting, disputes, etc.

Statutory Accounts: Statutory accounts are a vital part of running a limited company so that shareholders see how the company is performing. Statutory Accounts must be filed with Companies House annually.

SWOT Analysis: A SWOT analysis is a structured planning method used to evaluate the Strengths, Weaknesses, Opportunities, and Threats of a business venture.

A SWOT analysis involves specifying the objective of the business and identifying the internal and external factors that are favourable and unfavourable to achieving that objective.

VAT: The Value Added Tax, or VAT, is a general, broadly based consumption tax assessed on the value added to goods and services.

VAT Return: A VAT Return calculates how much VAT should be paid to, or reimbursed by, HM Revenue and Customs (HMRC). Returns are submitted four times a year.

Website: A website is a set of related web pages that promote the business, provide valuable information to site visitors, and offer 'precious' information in exchange for the visitor's contact details.

www.ingramcontent.com/pod-product-compliance
Lightning Source LLC
Chambersburg PA
CBHW060932140726
47996CB00001B/467